AF612399

THE HIDDEN WOUND OF REJECTION

THE HIDDEN WOUND OF REJECTION

The Truth That's Holding You Back

Gérson Dorneles

Text preparation, translation, editing,
cover design, and layout:
Gérson Dorneles

ISBN 978-65-01-38636-2

AUTHOR'S NOTE

In this book, I do not claim or intend to replace therapy or therapeutic treatments. I do not present myself as an expert in emotional trauma or a behavioral therapist. Above all, I am a learner on this vast journey of self-discovery that is life. My goal here is to share with you, someone who is also seeking answers, the experiences I've lived, the questions that guided me to the answers I found, and the tools I've learned to use and incorporate into my daily life to transform myself, and consequently, my life and my destiny.

I sincerely hope that the chapters of this book serve as a solid foundation, a push to help you see your own life from a new perspective, revealing the hidden truths within you. By bringing these truths to light, may you free yourself from the chains that have held back your highest flights, the ones your heart longs to reach.

ACKNOWLEDGMENTS

First and foremost, I thank God for granting me the grace to live this remarkable and extraordinary journey called life. I thank my parents, who have served as guides on this mission, and my grandparents, whose love and dedication accompanied me through my early experiences into my youth. To my wife, who is my muse and inspiration in every sense, I am deeply grateful for her unwavering support in every moment of our life together. To our children, for showing us the true meaning of life. And to all the people who, directly or indirectly, contributed to each step of my journey up to this point. May God bless all of you and reward you with the deepest desires of your hearts.

INTRODUCTION

A year ago, I felt like my life was falling apart. My work seemed stagnant, finances were a complete disaster, and my marriage was in ruins. I was on the brink of succumbing to despair. But, in the midst of this chaos, I stumbled upon something unexpected that would change everything. It's curious how this introduction may remind you of the beginning of a famous self-help book, but I can assure you that this is my truth— a personal and authentic experience that reflects what I truly went through.

I was on the edge, emotionally drained and lost in the middle of a storm of confusing thoughts and overwhelming emotions. Like Neale Donald Walsch in Conversations with God, I found myself immersed in existential questions, asking myself, "What does it take for life to truly work?" Where did I go wrong? How did I let my life get to this point, even though I had so many tools at my disposal? And most importantly, how could I change this trajectory?

Driven by these questions swirling in my mind, I began an unrelenting search for answers. The pages of books became my allies, and I dove into a phase of intense reading, absorbing knowledge with every new discovery. With each word I read, deep secrets about myself began to unfold. Hidden truths that had sabotaged my progress for so long emerged from the shadows. These revelations expanded my consciousness in ways I never imagined possible, lighting the way for the transformation I so desperately sought.

Now, I am here to share these discoveries with you. Because, if you're reading these words, you're likely on a similar path. I know you are also searching for answers, longing to uncover the truths hidden deep within you that have been holding you back from taking full control of your life. You want to face these truths head-on, confront them, and finally take control of your destiny.

If this is your desire, I have good news: you’re in the right place, at the right time, and with the right book. This is your moment to reveal what’s been hidden and rewrite your story. Let’s embark on this transformation journey together.

1

IDENTITY

What We Lose Along the Way

When we are born, we arrive in this world as complete beings, equipped with all the tools necessary to develop any skills we desire. We are pure potential, ready to explore, learn, and create. Our ability to be and do is limitless—this is our true essence, our identity.

The Bible tells us that we are made in the image and likeness of the Creator. Quantum physics suggests that we are observers who, by interacting with the quantum field, alter the reality around us. Regardless of the perspective you choose, one truth remains: in our original state, we possess the full potential to shape our lives according to our deepest desires.

But if we have all this, why do so many of us feel disconnected from this power? If we are naturally creative beings, why do we so often fail to build the life we dream of? Why does it seem like we are trapped in cycles of frustration and limitation? If we have the ability to change the world around us, why is it so difficult to change ourselves?

The answers to these questions are deeply rooted in the earliest years of our lives. As we grow, we absorb teachings from our parents, family, and the society around us. These experiences shape our values, rules, perspectives, and eventually, our behaviors. Traumatic experiences—or even seemingly small moments of humiliation and criticism that we interpret as rejection—can create barriers, slowly clipping our wings.

Over time, this continuous absorption of values, rules, and conditioning begins to limit our potential. Instead of staying connected to our authentic identity—the limitless essence we were born with—we start to drift away from it. It's as if our vast field of infinite possibilities gradually narrows as we adopt fears, insecurities, and limitations that were never truly ours. That expansive potential begins to shrink, and without realizing it, we start living on autopilot, responding to life's situations based on patterns we don't even know exist.

As the years pass, we become so disconnected from our true identity that, at some point, we lose the ability to answer even the simplest questions: Who am I, really? What do I truly want in life? Not in a philosophical sense, but in the most personal and practical way. What are your dreams? What truly makes your heart come alive? In many cases, the answers to these questions are buried beneath layers of conditioning we have accumulated throughout our lives.

But here's the good news: we can reverse this process. We can rediscover our true identity and reclaim our innate potential. To do this, we need to understand how the brain works and how it creates patterns to handle different aspects of life. This is where the concept of autopilot comes in, which we will explore next. Many of our daily actions are driven by automatic patterns formed through past experiences. And these patterns do not always reflect who we truly are. Let's examine how this happens—and, more importantly, what we can do to take back control.

Your life is running on autopilot!

Our brain is the most powerful and complex machine we know. Like an extraordinary manager, one of its primary functions is to optimize resources. This means seeking efficiency, speed, and, above all, conserving energy. To understand how this works, imagine the following scenario:

Every time we learn a new skill, our brain records each step of that learning process and creates an internal "*routine*"—a set of specific instructions and information for that particular skill. From that moment on, whenever we need to repeat the task, the brain activates this routine to execute it automatically, allowing the rest of the brain to focus on other activities.

Take learning to walk as an example. When you were a child, you took your first steps with great difficulty, stumbling and falling. With each attempt, your brain was there, monitoring every detail, adjusting, and refining your balance until, finally, you mastered the art of walking. At that point, the brain stored the entire process in a routine. Now, every time you stand up to walk, this routine is triggered, enabling you to move without even thinking about it. Your brain is free to focus on other things—like talking, planning your day, or reflecting on life—while you walk on autopilot.

But here's the key: the "*routine*" your brain uses to walk is the same one you created when you were just one year old! This means that, in terms of walking, you are still operating with the same basic instructions you acquired as a child. And this parallel applies to many other areas of your life.

Just like walking, running, talking, reading, writing, driving, and playing video games, there are hundreds of other tasks in our repertoire that we perform automatically. It is estimated that by the age of 30, 95% of our lives are already running on autopilot, while only 5% of our decisions are made consciously. That's why we often find ourselves wondering, "*How did I get here?*" or "*What have I done with my life?*"

Now, think about the impact of this when it comes to emotions. Imagine that, as a child, you experienced an intense emotional event that taught your brain how to react in a certain situation. If that learning was never updated, the routine that handles that emotion is still the one created when you were young—with the same limited resources and worldview you had at that age. Every time you encounter a similar situation in adulthood, that childhood routine takes control, reacting in the same way it learned back then.

* In programming language, a ***routine*** is a set of instructions or operations grouped into a function, method, or procedure that performs a specific task within a program. These routines are created so that certain operations can be reused multiple times in different parts of the code, without the programmer having to rewrite the same block of instructions repeatedly.

When I understood this dynamic, I realized how much our behaviors and emotional reactions are trapped in the past. Often, we are repeating routines formed in childhood without realizing that we now have new tools, new information, and new emotional and cognitive abilities at our disposal as adults.

In the coming chapters, we will explore in greater depth how these routines created during childhood influence our adult lives, especially in situations of trauma. We will uncover how you can take control and reprogram these blocks of information so they reflect your present reality—not a version of you that no longer exists.

The hidden hides in the obvious

My parents divorced when I was just one year old. I was raised by my paternal grandparents, alongside my uncles and aunts, on a farm in a small town with only five thousand inhabitants. My childhood was peaceful, with the simplicity typical of country life. As I grew older, especially during my teenage years, I met many people who were also children of divorced parents. These people often expressed their pain and resentment, carrying deep trauma from the family split. However, I never felt that way. I never identified with those stories of young people rebelling, spending their lives searching for their biological parents, seeking answers about their origins.

Until I was sixteen, I had never met my biological mother, yet curiously, I had never felt the need to look for her. In my mind, I was fine. Compared to so many other stories about children of divorced parents, I considered myself psychologically balanced and healthy. I didn't see the weight that this event had on me. After all, I knew about the separation, I had always known, and it seemed that acceptance was a natural part of my life. What I didn't realize, however, was that precisely because it was "in plain sight"—because I was fully aware of what had happened and believed it didn't affect me—a complex structure of emotional "routines" was forming, shaping my beliefs, behaviors, and, most importantly, my perception of myself.

Only after turning fifty, when I questioned why my life didn't reflect the potential I had always felt within me, I began to see the presence of these "*routines*." That was when I realized just how much I had been running on autopilot, as I mentioned earlier. There were internal "*routines*"—emotional and behavioral patterns—that took over in critical moments, leading me to act in ways I wasn't even conscious of. My whole life, I thought I was fine. But in reality, I never was. I was living on autopilot, being guided by "*routines*" created in my childhood. These hidden wounds, born from an event where I felt rejected, created a parallel reality that distorted the course of my life.

This realization opened my eyes to how these deeply ingrained "*routines*" of rejection can unconsciously shape our entire existence. Although fictional, the story of George McFly, Marty's father in **Back to the Future**, powerfully illustrates how these "*routines*" can shape a life.

George McFly was a man who spent most of his life weighed down by a deep sense of rejection. In school, George was shy, insecure, and frequently bullied—especially by Biff Tannen, the school bully. George never knew how to deal with those feelings. He grew up with the belief that he wasn't good enough, that he didn't deserve attention or respect. These feelings of inadequacy followed him everywhere, shaping his personality and decisions without him even realizing it.

His shyness prevented him from expressing himself, and he always preferred to stay on the sidelines, avoiding attention. The truth was, George never believed in his own worth. He saw himself as someone destined for mediocrity, without the courage to stand up for himself or dream big. In school, the little interaction he had with Lorraine, the love of his life and future wife, was filled with awkwardness. He didn't win her over with confidence or charm, but by pure chance—when he was hit by her father's car. Lorraine, in turn, fell in love with the situation, with the sweetness and vulnerability he displayed, not necessarily with the man he truly was.

As the years passed, George carried this deep-seated insecurity into his adult life. He married Lorraine, had children, but remained stuck in a passive existence. He worked in a mediocre job with no prospects for growth, and at home, he lived in quiet submission, without a voice of his own. Lorraine, who had married the idea of a youthful romance, also settled into a monotonous life, devoid of passion or ambition. Biff, who had always bullied George, became his boss. He continued to intimidate George, now in the workplace, and not a day went by when George didn't feel powerless in front of him.

In many scenes, Biff appears ordering George to do his reports, complaining whenever something wasn't done to his liking, always asserting his authority. George would just smile nervously and agree to everything, never daring to stand up to Biff.

The breaking point

But everything started to change on the night when Marty McFly, his son, was accidentally transported back in time to the year 1955. There, Marty discovered his parents' youth and, upon observing George's life, realized how his father had been shaped by a lifetime of submission and insecurity. Marty, understanding that his own existence was at risk if he didn't bring George and Lorraine together, began encouraging his father to take actions he would never have dared to take on his own.

The turning point came on a night that could have been just another moment where George remained in the shadows. Lorraine, who had already started to show interest in Marty (without knowing he was her son), was attacked by Biff in a car in the school parking lot. Biff, as always, took advantage of those weaker than him and tried to impose his will on Lorraine. However, this time, something inside George changed. Encouraged by Marty to fight for what he wanted, George finally decided to act.

When George saw Biff trying to force himself on Lorraine in the car, he felt a rage he had never felt before. The rejection, the submission, the years of being treated as invisible—all of it built up into a single moment. George ran to the car, flung open the door, and, with a mix of fear and determination, shouted:

— "*Let her go, Biff!*" — His voice trembled, but he didn't back down.

Biff, of course, mocked him, just as he always did:

— "*Oh, it's you, McFly? Why don't you disappear like you always do?*"

But this time, George didn't run. When Biff tried to attack him, George, with all the strength accumulated from years of repression, threw a punch that knocked the bully to the ground. That decisive moment—this impulse for change—not only altered that night but changed the course of his entire life.

A transformed life

The movie Back to the Future shows Marty returning to his original time and finding a completely different reality. His father was no longer that shy, submissive man. When Marty entered the house, he was shocked to see George McFly, now a successful author, confident, with a straight posture and a gleam in his eyes that he had never seen before. Lorraine was happier, more energetic, and even Biff, the former oppressor, was now humbly working for George, washing the family car.

That moment when George faced Biff was the reprogramming of the "*routines*" that had shaped an entire life of hidden wound of rejection. From that point on, George began to believe in himself. He realized he didn't have to live in the shadow of others, that he had value, that he could achieve whatever he wanted. He began making decisions based on confidence, not fear. He decided to pursue his dreams and became a science fiction writer, something he had always wanted but never had the courage to admit.

His relationship with Lorraine also changed. Now, there was mutual respect. The love between them flourished in a way that would never have happened if George had remained stuck in his insecurities. He was no longer the passive, invisible husband. He was a partner, someone Lorraine admired and wanted to share her life with.

This transformation of George McFly powerfully illustrates the impact of the "*hidden wound of rejection*". For years, George lived a life dictated by theses wounds, without realizing how much they shaped his actions, his choices, and, consequently, his destiny. But when he finally took action, when he faced Biff and decided to fight for what he wanted, everything changed.

A simple act of courage was enough to alter the course of his entire life. This shows us that, by confronting and overcoming hidden wound of rejection, we can rewrite our own story. What seemed like a life destined for failure and mediocrity can be completely transformed with a single decision to reprogram the "*routines*" that keep us tied to the past. George McFly shows us that when we face our hidden wound of rejection, we open the door to a much brighter future full of possibilities.

2

ART IMITATES LIFE

Knowing the traumas is not enough

We all carry traumatic events throughout our lives, each with its own unique intensity. Although we are aware of most of these occurrences, even if only in a fragmented way, this knowledge alone is not enough to heal the wounds or free us from their effects. Some people manage to use these events as a springboard to grow and propel themselves forward, while others cling to them as justifications for repetitive and destructive behaviors. There are also many who believe they have not been affected by such events, yet they are intensely impacted on an unconscious level. However, the issue is not merely recognizing that these traumas existed. The real challenge lies in understanding the invisible side effects they have caused—those feelings and behaviors that operate covertly, shaping our decisions and altering the course of our lives, often without us realizing it.

During my own search for these hidden effects, I encountered an unexpected truth: many of these impacts did not stem from major traumas but from seemingly insignificant childhood events—episodes that, at first glance, did not appear to hold any importance. I remember recalling such moments and thinking, "*Really? This is what triggered these feelings and behaviors? What nonsense! How childish!*" And this is precisely where the key to understanding lies. These events, which could be considered mere "*childishness*," were emotionally intense enough to leave deep marks on my neural system.

Do you remember, in the first chapter, the analogy I made between our brain's synapses and the creation of "*routines*"? These "*routines*" function like automatic mental programs, designed to handle specific situations based on past learning. When something emotionally intense happens, the brain creates a neural association—a fast track that will be triggered in the future whenever a similar event occurs. And here lies the problem: the "*routine*" that responds at certain moments in our lives may not be our current, adult, and conscious version. Instead, it might be the 1-year-old, 5-year-old, or 10-year-old version of ourselves when that pattern was first created.

This is why, at times, friends or family members may accuse us of "*acting like a child*" in certain situations. While this criticism may sound offensive, there is some truth to it. When these old "*routines*" take control, what is really happening is that we are allowing the child we once were—still immature and emotionally unprepared—to take the reins of our decisions. We do not do this consciously, but automatically, just as we drive a car, ride a bike, or type without thinking.

These behaviors and feelings are deeply embedded in the brain's "*routines*," ready to be triggered whenever a situation even slightly similar to the original event arises. However, unlike practical skills such as driving or speaking, these emotional patterns can sabotage us, creating a constant repetition of outdated and inappropriate reactions for our current stage in life.

Thus, merely knowing that we have experienced traumatic events is not enough. Simply recognizing these experiences does not make us fully aware of the neural associations that were formed in response to them. More importantly, this superficial knowledge does not disable the "*autopilot*" that allows old patterns to continue shaping our present.

A deep and meticulous investigation is required—one that goes beyond merely recalling the events themselves. It involves carefully observing our daily behaviors, our emotional reactions to trivial situations, and our automatic responses to challenges. *Where do these reactions originate? Which "routine" is taking control at those moments?* By conducting this analysis, we begin to recognize that, in many instances, we are not reacting as our mature, adult selves but rather as the wounded child carrying distorted and incomplete memories of the past.

This investigative process allows us to look at past events from a new perspective. We are now adults, equipped with more emotional and cognitive tools. Time has granted us the ability to revisit these episodes and understand them differently. This means we can reinterpret traumatic events—or even those that were not overtly traumatic but left deep marks—and begin to create new "*routines*."

These new "*routines*" will gradually replace the old ones that were based on hidden wounds of rejection. By doing so, we start reclaiming control over our lives and decisions, taking back the reins that, for so long, were in the hands of an outdated version of ourselves.

The journey of self-discovery that this investigation provides is both liberating and challenging. It requires courage to revisit painful memories and to question long-standing behavioral patterns that have seemed unquestionable for so long. However, the reward of this pursuit is priceless: reconnecting with your original identity—the one that was obscured by "*routines*" of pain and wounds of rejection.

Just like in fiction (*George McFly*), in real life, you also have the power to rewrite your story. You can face your wounds of rejection, your traumas, and your failures, and emerge stronger. You can choose to no longer allow childhood "*routines*" to continue guiding your life. Instead, you can build new neural pathways that will lead you toward a future of fulfillment and freedom—a future where your deepest dreams, once hidden in the shadows of the hidden wound of rejection, can finally emerge and be revealed in the light of self-awareness.

PART I

Know yourself

Socrates

3

REJECTION

The word "*rejection*" comes from the Latin *reiectio*, derived from the verb *reicere*, which literally means "*to throw back*" or "*to refuse.*" From its very origin, rejection is simply that: a refusal, a redirection. Something that is not accepted at the moment. But does rejection alone truly wound or leave deep scars?

If we take a moment to reflect, we'll realize that we face rejection daily. It's a part of life. We all say and hear "*no*" constantly. Think about your daily routine: if you work as a salesperson or a telemarketer, for example, "*no*" is a word you encounter all the time. And for those on the other end of the call, saying "*no*" is just as normal—whether to an offer, a proposal, or any type of request.

We reject things without even noticing: when we say no to our children, our parents, our partners, or when we turn down a request at work. Likewise, we are also rejected—when applying for a job, when trying to win someone over, or when a personal project isn't accepted.

Now, take a moment to think: how many times have you been rejected today? This week? This month? And how many of those rejections left a lasting mark on you? The truth is that the vast majority of these "*no's*" don't cause real pain. They are simply part of life's flow, like a current that sometimes pushes us in another direction. They are not attacks on our worth but rather choices made by others—often based on their own circumstances rather than something we did wrong.

Rejection, by itself, does not cause pain. If rejection were the primary cause of trauma or emotional wounds, life would be unbearable. The reality is that most of the "*no's*" we receive daily barely affect us. They are part of the natural ebb and flow of interactions and opportunities. The pain we feel doesn't come from rejection itself, but from something much deeper that follows: the wound of rejection.

It is this wound—our personal interpretation of the experience—that has the power to cause emotional wounds. When rejection touches our insecurities, when we perceive it as a reflection of our worth, it turns into suffering. And that is precisely what we will explore next...

The Wound of Rejection

It is not what happens to us, but how we react.

Epictetus – Greek philosopher

The pain of rejection does not lie in the act of being rejected itself. The proof of this is that the same "NO" may mean nothing to one person, while for another, it feels like the end of the world. Observe how this happens all the time: how often have you tried to console someone suffering from rejection that, in your view, wasn't so significant, yet to that person, it felt like a catastrophe? And the opposite is also true: how many times have you suffered over something that, to others, didn't seem like a big deal? In these situations, you might think they don't understand your pain because they didn't experience it themselves. But the truth is that, for those people, the event would not have caused the same pain it did for you. The answer lies in the meaning we assign to these experiences.

As the saying goes: "*Things have no meaning except the one we give them.*" Our interpretation of events defines their impact on us, shaped by the emotional history each of us carries.

We can affirm that the pain of rejection is not about the present event but about a much older wound, buried in our past. Something happened at a certain point in our lives, likely in childhood or adolescence, leaving such a deep emotional mark that, ever since, we have been in a constant state of alert. This is the true enemy: the hidden wound of rejection.

During our early years, just as our bodies are growing and developing, our emotional and cognitive resources necessary to interpret or contextualize situations mature as well. Unlike adulthood, where we can rationalize and understand that people's behaviors are influenced by numerous external factors, as children, we interpret events much more literally and personally. A criticism or exclusion is quickly perceived as a personal failure rather than a reflection of another situation. Without the emotional maturity to distinguish between what is internal and external, we tend to interpret "NO's," criticisms, and the natural challenges of social interactions as direct rejections of our essence rather than as part of an external context or temporary situations.

Thus, the hidden wound of rejection forms when our sense of identity is still in full development. Since this sense of identity is largely built through our interactions with those around us, the opinions and validation of important figures such as parents, teachers, and friends shape our self-perception and self-worth. When this validation is absent or negative, our brain begins to create the "*routines*" of the hidden wound of rejection.

This wound, though hidden, functions just like an open wound when you get physically hurt. The intense pain in the injured area makes you react instantly and excessively to any threat of contact. Your body develops automatic reflexes to protect the wounded area. The same happens with emotional wounds: the brain programs itself to avoid any possibility of feeling that pain again, no matter how unlikely it may be. It is always on alert, watching and preventing anything that could be interpreted as a threat.

Think of an event where you felt intensely rejected. A situation where you were not accepted or were criticized by someone whose love or approval you sought. It might have been a word spoken at a crucial moment, a lack of attention during a moment of vulnerability, or even a decision that made you feel inferior or excluded. From that moment on, your brain created a "*routine*"—a sort of emotional guardian—on duty 24/7, ready to prevent you from reliving that pain. And just as the body protects a burn, your emotional system reacts to any situation that even remotely resembles that original event.

At the time this event occurred, you did not have the tools to fully understand or contextualize the reasons behind the rejection. That's why it was interpreted as something so painful, creating such a significant emotional wound that your brain formed this "*routine*." The detail is that, even though years have passed and you now possess far greater cognitive and emotional tools than you did when that event took place, this "*routine*" continues operating under the same original programming. If that event had never happened and only occurred now, you would handle it completely differently. So why, when facing something similar today, does your entire body react as it did before? The answer lies in the "*routine*" designed to deal with the situation. It has not been updated; it still functions with the same tools it had when it was first programmed. This is why current events can trigger such deep pain.

That's why, at certain moments, a "*simple NO*" in everyday life can trigger a disproportionate emotional reaction. What is happening is not just about the current event but about an emotional memory from the past. The brain connects the dots, activates the "*routine*," and puts you in defense mode. This can happen in any area of life—relationships, work, friendships. Suddenly, you feel deeply affected by something that, rationally, you know shouldn't have so much power over you. But the truth is, it's not the present event that is hurting you—it's the old, still open and sensitive wound that has been touched.

This is why we suffer from certain rejections and not others. We are not suffering because of the present, but because of the hidden memory of a rejection that was never fully processed or healed. The real pain comes from that "*original event*," the specific moment that marked the beginning of this emotional journey.

Understanding this was liberating. Not because the pain disappeared instantly, but because, in identifying the source, I began to realize that present-day rejections don't actually hold the power I once believed. They were not the cause of my suffering, just the triggers that activated an older pain.

Now that we understand how the wound of rejection manifests, we need to explore its many facets. The wound of rejection does not only present itself through the obvious pain of an explicit "NO." It is disguised, hiding in behaviors we adopt to protect ourselves from rejection: perfectionism, isolation, constant validation-seeking, fear of exposure, or fear of truly connecting with others. These and other behaviors are "*routines*" the brain has programmed to prevent that old wound from being touched again.

The Hidden Wound of Rejection

" Until you make the unconscious conscious, it will direct your life and you will call it fate."

Carl Jung

Once the hidden wound of rejection takes root, it intertwines deeply with our emotions and behaviors, automatically controlling our reactions and decisions. Over the years, this feeling unconsciously shapes us, becoming so ingrained and habitual that it starts to blend with our personality. We go through life believing that our reactions, thoughts, and emotions are intrinsic to our identity, without realizing that, more often than not, these aspects are governed by a deep-seated fear rather than our authentic essence.

Unfortunately, we can go years, or even a lifetime, without realizing that we have been shaped by this hidden wound of rejection. It disguises itself, taking the form of behavioral patterns that we believe to be part of who we are. After all, it is difficult to distinguish what is truly part of our nature from what is merely the result of this underlying fear. We assume that the way we act, feel, and react is simply "*who we are*," making it much harder to recognize that something might be amiss.

Often, only as the years pass and we repeatedly face suffering, frustration, or stagnation do we begin to question ourselves in a deeper and more constructive way. When we notice that certain negative patterns keep repeating—so intensely that they force us to stop and reflect—we start to suspect that something beyond our conscious awareness is shaping our lives. This cycle of events, often challenging and painful, can serve as the "*wake-up call*" we need. At this point, we start asking ourselves: *Am I under some kind of spell? Is there a demon keeping me from living my dreams?* Or *is it the envy of my neighbors holding me back?* These and countless other questions arise until, in a moment of greater clarity and self-confrontation, a more crucial question emerges: *Am I re-*

ally like this, or am I acting unconsciously, based on outdated brain patterns that no longer align with my present adult self, who has better knowledge and cognitive tools?

This process of self-reflection reveals something essential: beneath our defense mechanisms, we are much more than we believe ourselves to be. We discover that our ability to live and thrive is limited by beliefs formed from the hidden wound of rejection, which keeps us trapped in a repetitive cycle.

Once we become aware of this, inevitable questions arise: *How can we identify this hidden wound of rejection? How can we distinguish between our true personality and what is merely a defense mechanism disguised as self-preservation?* These questions are crucial to the process of self-awareness and transformation. Only when we begin to separate what is authentic within us from what is an automatic fear response can we take control of our choices and live fully.

In the next chapter, we will explore how childhood experiences interpreted as rejection can shape our behaviors, decisions, and relationships in adulthood. We will examine how these emotional wounds, often silent, influence the way we respond to vulnerability and affect our interpersonal interactions. The goal is to bring to light behavioral patterns that, even without realizing it, carry the marks of the hidden wound of rejection, helping you identify these signs in your own life. By deepening this understanding, you will see how these past wounds still exert an unseen influence over your choices and perceptions, creating a cycle of automatic responses that can distort your true essence and limit your personal growth.

4

HOW THE HIDDEN WOUND OF REJECTION SHAPES OUR LIVES

As we have already discussed, during childhood—the stage of emotional formation—we are unable to interpret the complexity of events in which we are criticized, compared, mocked, abandoned, or exposed to undesirable situations. We perceive these experiences literally and personally, as direct rejection. It is within this context that the Hidden wound of rejection is born, giving rise to a set of behaviors that manifest in all areas of our lives. These behaviors act both preventively and defensively, aiming to protect us from any threat that might aggravate our emotional wound.

Some behaviors become more predominant than others, depending on how the original wound of rejection was created and evolved over time. To deepen this analysis, I have identified seven behavioral patterns that shape our lives: Self-image and self-esteem, Need for control and security, Ability to build relationships, Procrastination and performance, Emotional reactivity and regulation, Distrust and toxic relationships, and Self-expression and creativity.

We will analyze each of these patterns across different aspects of life. By identifying them, it will be easier to trace their origins, allowing for a deeper understanding and, ultimately, the reprogramming of the emotional "*routines*" that govern our behaviors.

At the end of each section, you will find a self-reflection exercise with guiding questions for you to ask yourself. The goal is to uncover evidence that a hidden wound of rejection may be shaping and directing your life. Take your time with these questions. Be open and sincere so that your answers come from the depths of your true SELF. It is crucial that you pause your reading to dedicate a moment to reflect on the proposed questions.

Grab a notebook and write down everything that comes to mind. Writing is a powerful tool for bringing hidden memories, feelings, and sensations to the surface. By putting your thoughts on paper, you gain greater clarity and depth in your reflections. This process helps you identify patterns and better understand how certain experiences have shaped your behavior.

It is human nature to recognize these behavioral patterns more easily in others than in ourselves. That is why honesty is essential in your search for self-awareness. Only by tearing down the veil of the EGO can you truly see what lies hidden within.

SELF-IMAGE AND SELF-ESTEEM

The set of behaviors related to Self-Image and Self-Esteem is formed by the hidden wound of rejection originating from experiences of negative comparisons, constant criticism, and public humiliation. It directly affects how a person perceives themselves, influencing their self-esteem and self-perception.

Low Self-esteem

When the hidden wound of rejection originates from experiences of constant comparison and devaluation, it directly impacts self-esteem. The defense mechanism created in response is low self-esteem. To avoid the pain of repeated comparisons and feelings of worthlessness, the brain begins to perceive itself as inferior and incapable. It adopts the belief that "*I am not good enough,*" reasoning that if we are already "*on the ground,*" no one can knock us down further.

According to Freud, defense mechanisms are unconscious strategies we use to avoid emotional pain. By internalizing the belief that we are "*less than*", the ego attempts to shield itself from further blows, convincing itself that staying down will prevent future disappointments. However, this defense becomes a psychological prison. Instead of protecting us, it reinforces a cycle of self-sabotage, shaping our self-worth and distorting our perception of reality. Each time we experience comparison or devaluation, the pain feels less intense—not because we are truly unaffected, but because we have accepted inferiority as our truth.

This protective mechanism deeply influences our behaviors. The idea of inferiority takes root, and any situation that exposes us to judgment or evaluation triggers the cycle of self-sabotage. We convince ourselves that staying small, avoiding recognition, and steering clear of confrontation will protect us from rejection. After all, if we already believe we are not enough, negative feedback or criticism will seem less painful.

On a subconscious level, this pattern reinforces a distorted self-image. Fear of failure or judgment leads us to avoid situations where our abilities might be tested. Anxiety over potential comparisons becomes constant, and our behavior adapts to minimize exposure: we avoid public speaking, decline opportunities, and even in personal relationships, we withdraw and adopt a reserved stance.

This cycle traps us. Instead of growing and exploring our true potential, we remain stuck in the belief that we are not enough. The subconscious, in its attempt to protect us from rejection, reinforces the narrative of inferiority, pushing us further away from opportunities for fulfillment and growth. The fear of rejection confines us to self-imposed limits, where the false safety of mediocrity shields us from pain—but also prevents us from evolving.

Excessive Self-criticism

When the hidden wound of rejection arises from constant criticism, it can trigger a pattern of excessive self-criticism. The defense mechanism created in response is a relentless need for self-correction and an unending pursuit of perfection. In this process, the brain attempts to avoid the pain of external criticism and judgment by developing a hyper-awareness of its own flaws, convincing itself that the only way to prevent further rejection is to be flawless. This leads to the belief that even the smallest mistake completely compromises personal worth.

This defensive pattern quickly becomes a trap. In *The Ego and the Mechanisms of Defense*, Anna Freud describes how the ego, in an attempt to anticipate external threats, internalizes criticism and develops a continuous, punitive self-surveillance. This process, known as "*identification with the aggressor,*" causes individuals to internalize critical voices, making them part of their own self-awareness. This internalized defense constantly seeks to predict and prevent mistakes. As self-criticism intensifies with every error or external judgment, it reinforces the idea that no matter how hard we try, we will never be good enough.

This constant anticipation of criticism shapes our actions and decisions, ultimately blocking our growth. We become afraid to take risks or try new things out of fear of not being perfect. Excessive self-criticism not only reinforces a distorted self-image but also paralyzes our ability to take initiative, making us choose the safety of avoiding possible mistakes over the challenge of failing and facing criticism.

As Anna Freud suggests, this seemingly protective defense ultimately imprisons us. Instead of safeguarding our self-esteem, the cycle of self-criticism distances us from true self-confidence and traps us in an endless quest for external validation. The fear of disapproval prevents us from fully expressing ourselves and embracing new experiences, limiting our potential and keeping us from living a more fulfilling and authentic life.

Impostor Syndrome

When the hidden wound of rejection stems from a lack of recognition or validation, the defense mechanism we develop is Impostor Syndrome. Even when we are highly competent or accomplished in our fields, we struggle to internalize our successes and live in constant fear of being exposed as a "*fraud.*" This mechanism convinces us that our value or competence will never be enough, creating an unconscious strategy to avoid the pain of waiting for recognition that never comes.

From an early age, the lack of recognition for our achievements and efforts can take root in us, reinforcing the belief that no matter what we do, we will never truly be seen or valued. This phenomenon is particularly noticeable in households where praise or validation is rare, where success is considered the "*bare minimum*" expected, or in environments that focus only on mistakes rather than achievements. Such family dynamics play a significant role in the development of impostor syndrome, as the lack of validation from childhood strengthens the idea that our worth depends on external circumstances rather than our own merits. Growing up in this type of environment, we internalize the message that our competence, effort, and skills will never be enough to earn recognition.

Instead of believing that success results from our dedication and effort, we begin to think that if we succeed, it was merely due to luck, coincidence, or some misunderstanding that will eventually be uncovered. This psychological defense mechanism serves as emotional protection: if we convince ourselves that success is accidental or undeserved, we try to shield ourselves from the pain of rejection caused by unmet expectations of recognition. By never allowing ourselves to believe that we are truly capable, we, in theory, never feel devastated by the lack of validation or praise that we believe we do not deserve.

In adulthood, this pattern manifests as chronic insecurity, even in the face of remarkable achievements. Impostor Syndrome makes us feel like we are "*deceiving*" others about our true abilities. Every success we attain is seen as an exception rather than a reflection of our competence, leading us into a cycle of self-sabotage, fear, and anxiety. The more we achieve, the greater our fear of being "*discovered.*" This mechanism, which was originally meant to protect us from the pain of not being recognized, ends up limiting us, preventing us from feeling satisfaction or pride in our progress.

One of the most insidious aspects of Impostor Syndrome is that it can arise in any area of our lives—at work, in personal relationships, in academics, and even in hobbies or leisure activities. A talented professional may feel like they do not belong in their workplace, even after multiple promotions. A student who consistently gets good grades may believe their success is due to luck or that teachers have simply not noticed their flaws. Even in relationships, we may feel unworthy of love or appreciation, always fearing that the other person will "*discover*" who we truly are and be disappointed.

This defense pattern is reinforced by a constant pursuit of perfection and a fear of making mistakes. Since we believe we are not naturally competent, we try to compensate with extra work, excessive dedication, and relentless self-pressure. The idea of making a mistake or receiving criticism feels like a direct threat to our identity because we already live with the sensation that we are about to be "*exposed*" as incompetent. This cycle of anxiety and insecurity strengthens the feeling of being an impostor, perpetuating the belief that success will never be deserved or secure.

Ultimately, Impostor Syndrome traps us in a spiral of insecurity, limiting our growth and preventing us from truly enjoying our achievements.

Personal Shame

When the wound of rejection manifests as a result of public humiliation, the defense mechanism we develop is personal shame. Shame becomes a self-protection strategy, leading us to avoid situations where we might be exposed, criticized, or ridiculed again. This feeling arises as a response to the fear of being judged and humiliated once more and, in many cases, profoundly shapes our behavior.

These experiences of public humiliation can have roots in various moments throughout life. In childhood, events such as being ridiculed at school can leave lasting scars; in adulthood, situations like failing a presentation or being publicly criticized by someone in a position of authority can intensify this emotional wound. These occurrences leave a deep impact, leading the mind to develop mechanisms to avoid any exposure that might bring another humiliating experience.

In our attempt to protect ourselves from the pain of shame, we often limit our choices and actions. As John Bradshaw observes in his book Healing the Shame That Binds You: "*Toxic shame becomes part of our identity. Instead of thinking 'I made a mistake,' we start to believe that we are a mistake.*" This internalization distorts our self-perception, transforming the fear of making mistakes into the fear of simply being. The result is constant and severe self-censorship, which restricts our freedom of expression and personal growth.

This cycle of self-control prevents us from acting with authenticity—we adjust our behavior to meet others' expectations or to avoid the risk of public failure. Shame places us in a defensive position, where we avoid standing out or expressing ourselves fully, always fearing another humiliation.

Over time, this continuous self-protection process distorts our perception of ourselves. Bradshaw emphasizes that personal shame ultimately isolates us: "*Toxic shame is the underlying feeling that creates emotional isolation. It keeps us from connecting with others and with ourselves.*" This emotional isolation further fuels shame, making us wary of social interactions and reluctant to establish genuine connections, which only strengthens the cycle of withdrawal.

In our closest relationships, this fear of being devalued translates into difficulty in being vulnerable. Shame causes us to avoid emotional openness for fear that our flaws will be exposed, so we create a façade of perfection to protect ourselves from rejection. However, by hiding, we also deprive ourselves of authentic connections and the intimacy that genuine relationships offer.

Over time, this defense mechanism, originally created to avoid pain, becomes an anchor that holds us back from growth and exploring our potential. When we are trapped in shame, we continuously question our self-worth and believe that the only way to avoid humiliation is to hide from the world.

Pause to Reflect

Take a moment to reflect on the behavioral patterns that shape your self-image and self-esteem. Answer the following questions with sincerity, and remember: many answers emerge over time, in moments of greater calm and introspection.

1) *Do I often compare myself to others, feeling inferior, even without clear evidence to justify it?*

- When I see friends or colleagues achieving milestones such as promotions, trips, or personal accomplishments, do I feel like my own life loses value?
- Do I avoid sharing my experiences or projects because I think they are not good enough compared to others?
- Are there moments when I struggle to appreciate what I have, simply because I am focused on other people's achievements?

2) *Do I have difficulty accepting compliments and recognition for my effort and competence?*

- When someone praises me, do I minimize my accomplishment by saying "*it was just luck*", "*simple*", or "*not a big deal*"?
- Do I feel like I don't deserve the recognition I receive, attributing my successes to circumstances or the help of others?
- Do I prefer to deflect attention from a compliment, believing that I am not as good as others think?

3) *Do I avoid exposing myself or trying something new out of fear of judgment, mistakes, or failure?*

- Am I afraid to participate in social or professional activities because I believe I will be criticized or humiliated?
- Do I give up on personal projects or dreams because I think I'm not capable or that people will notice my flaws?
- Do I prefer to stay in my comfort zone to avoid the risk of being negatively evaluated?

4) *Am I too hard on myself when I make small mistakes that others probably wouldn't even notice?*

- When I make a mistake, do I spend too much time thinking about it and mentally punishing myself?
- Do I feel like small details define my worth or competence, even if no one else notices them?
- Do I repeatedly review my actions or decisions, fearing that I did something wrong?

Next, I will share a personal experience to illustrate how reflective exercises and journaling can uncover feelings and behaviors that once went unnoticed. By doing the same, you may access parts of yourself that have been waiting for the opportunity to come to light.

Ice Skating

When I was in high school, I had morning classes, and two or three times a week, I would meet up with some friends to go to the mall. It was a routine for us—we would spend hours talking, laughing, and watching people pass by. That mall had a permanent ice-skating rink, and we often stood by the glass, watching people take risks, fall, laugh, get up, and try again. My friends always got excited, rented skates, went onto the rink, fell, and had fun. But I—I never allowed myself to step in.

At the time, I believed my hesitation was shyness. An inner voice whispered incessantly: *"They already know how to skate, and you've never even stepped on an ice rink. You'll fall on your first try, barely putting your feet down. Can you imagine the embarrassment of falling in front of everyone? Getting your clothes wet, looking awkward while people laugh at you, watching you struggle just to stand? And then, how will you get home all wet, taking the bus, with that lingering feeling of failure?"*

And without questioning it, I obeyed that voice. I had countless opportunities to experience that moment alongside my friends—to dive into the adventure, to laugh at the falls, and to celebrate small victories—but I let them all slip away. I never stepped onto the ice.

Now, as I write these lines and reflect on the questions I've posed to myself, this memory has resurfaced, bringing with it a feeling of regret. It's astonishing how a small decision, influenced by an irrational fear or a *"routine"* programmed in childhood, can deprive us of moments that could have been deeply meaningful. This memory made me realize how much I have missed out on—not because I didn't want to, but because I feared judgment, because of a sense of inadequacy that, in reality, never had any real foundation.

Today, with a new perspective, I've decided that ice skating is something I will still do. I've added it to my list of things to accomplish before I die. Because, in the end, it's not just about skating. It's about challenging the voice that has limited me for so long.

In the coming chapters, as we delve deeper into other sets of behaviors and emotions, you will gain a clearer understanding of the hidden rejection patterns that have influenced your life. This will help you trace the origins of these wounds and mark the beginning of your journey to freedom.

5

NEED FOR CONTROL AND SECURITY

The need for control and security is a defense mechanism created by hidden wound of rejection, often rooted in instability or vulnerability experienced throughout life. When we face situations where we feel helpless, criticized, or incapable of influencing the events around us, the urge to control our surroundings can intensify as a way to restore a sense of security.

This desire for control doesn't just manifest in major decisions–it also influences small, everyday aspects of life. It is driven by subconscious fears of reliving traumatic experiences, such as family instability, constant criticism, or lack of emotional support. As a result, various behaviors emerge, all based on the need to maintain control–whether over oneself, others, or circumstances.

Within this set of behaviors, we find excessive control, perfectionism, obsessive tendencies, exaggerated self-sufficiency, and inflexibility. Each of these patterns represents a way of coping with the wound of rejection, and they are all interconnected by the underlying need to protect emotional integrity and prevent further rejection or destabilization.

Obsessive Behavior and Excessive Control

When hidden wound of rejection stems from experiences of family instability, obsessive behavior and excessive control emerge as defense mechanisms to cope with chaos and a lack of stability in our homes. This instability can manifest in many ways: the absence of clear rules, unpredictable changes, constant conflicts, or the inability of authority figures to provide emotional leadership. In response to such instability, we try to compensate for our feelings of powerlessness and vulnerability by attempting to control our environment, the people around us, and even ourselves.

This need for control goes beyond a simple desire for organization—it is born from a desperate need for security. In unstable environments, any unpredictability is perceived as an emotional threat. As a result, we create rigid and repetitive patterns that give us the illusion of stability. In childhood, this may manifest as obsessively keeping our room perfectly tidy or creating strict routines. In adolescence, it may appear as an obsession with perfect grades or physical appearance. These behaviors are attempts to minimize the chaos around us and avoid rejection.

Chaotic family environments share a common element: a lack of security. When we grow up in unpredictable situations or with inconsistent authority figures, we internalize the idea that we must control everything within our reach to feel safe. As children and teenagers, we begin to regulate our behavior in extreme ways to compensate for external instability.

With excessive control, the need to manage every detail turns into an obsession. At work, this may manifest as micromanaging projects or trying to anticipate every variable to prevent mistakes. In relationships, it can take the form of wanting to regulate a partner's actions and emotions, fearing that their independence could lead to emotional instability. Obsessive behavior, on the other hand, appears as repetitive rituals—constantly checking something, maintaining extreme organization, or meticulously planning every action. Both behaviors stem from the same fear: reliving the emotional chaos of the past.

Excessive control and obsessive behavior generate anxiety, stress, and a cycle of frustration, as reality is naturally unpredictable and no control is absolute. These behaviors also damage our relationships by distancing us from intimacy and trust, and they limit our personal growth by preventing us from embracing new experiences or accepting mistakes as part of learning.

The constant attempt to control everything leaves us exhausted and reinforces our sense of powerlessness. Over time, these patterns become emotional prisons, preventing us from living with ease, embracing life's uncertainties, and achieving true emotional freedom.

Perfectionism

" Perfectionism is not the same as striving for excellence. It is the belief that if we look perfect, live perfectly, and do everything perfectly, we can minimize or avoid the pain of judgment and shame."
Brené Brown

When the wound of rejection stems from constant criticism, the defense mechanism that develops—beyond excessive self-criticism—is perfectionism. This mechanism convinces us that to avoid rejection, we must perform everything flawlessly, without mistakes, and meet others' expectations. The criticism we receive throughout life, whether from parents, teachers, or authority figures, shapes our belief that the only path to acceptance and recognition is through perfection. Thus, perfectionism takes hold as a shield against the fear of being criticized or rejected again.

Living under the weight of continuous criticism fosters an overwhelming need to avoid any errors, no matter how small. The pressure to be impeccable starts to govern our actions. Over time, the pursuit of perfection becomes an obsession where even the slightest mistake feels like a threat to our acceptance. What we fail to realize is that this pattern creates an exhausting cycle—one in which we are constantly striving for an unattainable ideal.

Despite being seen by some as a virtue, perfectionism carries a heavy emotional burden. It prevents us from relaxing, accepting our limitations, and acknowledging that we are human—therefore, fallible. It makes us believe that if we are perfect, the criticism will stop, and we will finally be accepted. However, perfectionism never grants us this longed-for peace. On the contrary, the more we chase perfection, the greater the pressure to maintain impossible standards.

In many cases, perfectionism also paralyzes us. The fear of failure prevents us from taking action. We postpone projects, avoid new opportunities, and refuse to take risks because we are afraid the outcome won't be perfect. This behavior affects not only our professional goals but also our personal relationships, as the need for control and external validation distances us from genuine and spontaneous experiences.

The impact of perfectionism can be devastating to our self-esteem. When we focus only on avoiding criticism and judgment, we begin to measure our worth based on our achievements and the absence of mistakes. When we do make mistakes—no matter how small—we feel defeated and inadequate, reinforcing the cycle of self-imposed pressure and harsh self-criticism.

Additionally, perfectionism isolates us. We build a barrier between ourselves and others, fearing that if they see our flaws, they will judge and reject us. The belief that we must be flawless in every aspect of life prevents us from asking for help, delegating tasks, and trusting others. We want to project an image of efficiency and competence at all times, yet by doing so, we deny ourselves a lighter and more authentic way of living.

This behavioral pattern traps us in an unrealistic expectation. We try to escape the criticism that shaped us in the past, but in doing so, we become our own harshest critics. Perfectionism blinds us to the truth—that genuine acceptance comes from embracing our flaws and imperfections.

Excessive Self-Sufficiency

Excessive self-sufficiency is a defense mechanism developed when the hidden wound of rejection stems from a lack of support. When, during childhood or adolescence, we feel that we cannot rely on others—whether due to a lack of emotional support, neglect, or even excessive responsibilities imposed on us too early—we learn to trust only ourselves. Self-sufficiency becomes a heavy burden, preventing us from asking for help and isolating us emotionally. This behavior arises as a form of self-protection, but over time, it leads us to a state of disconnection from others and from our own vulnerabilities.

Growing up in an environment where there is no room for mistakes or dependence forces us to develop excessive self-sufficiency to cope with the absence of support. This can manifest in several ways. Imagine a child who, when facing difficulties at school, does not receive the necessary help from their parents—whether due to lack of time, interest, or simple neglect. This child learns that, in order to overcome challenges, they can only rely on themselves. At the same time, they feel rejected because their emotional and practical needs are not being met.

Another common example occurs when, during youth, we are forced to take on adult responsibilities too soon. Perhaps because our parents or caregivers are absent, emotionally or physically, we end up being "*parents*" to ourselves or even to our siblings. Under these circumstances, the emotional support that should have been a solid foundation during our development is missing. This forces us to develop a rigid stance of self-sufficiency, believing that any dependence or fragility will only make us more vulnerable.

The bigger problem arises when this excessive self-sufficiency carries over into adulthood. We begin to reject any form of help, believing that accepting support is a sign of weakness. In our careers, we may refuse to delegate tasks, taking on the entire workload because we believe that no one else will do things as well as we do. In relationships, we avoid sharing our emotional struggles or asking for help, fearing that we will appear weak or incapable. This isolates us even further, reinforcing the false belief that we are alone in the world and that the only way to survive is to rely solely on our own strength.

Excessive self-sufficiency also prevents us from forming deep emotional connections. By building a barrier of independence, we deny ourselves the opportunity for vulnerability, which is essential for healthy human relationships. The fear of being rejected when asking for help leads us to create a façade of unshakable strength, even when, deep down, we may be exhausted and anxious. The irony is that in trying to protect our vulnerability, we end up perpetuating a cycle of isolation, where we are unable to truly connect with others.

A clear example of this can be seen in a young man who, after being ignored by his parents during difficult moments in adolescence, begins to believe that depending on someone is a mistake. He grows into an adult who trusts no one to help solve his problems and prefers to face everything alone, even at the cost of his mental peace and health. Similarly, a person who never received adequate emotional support as a child may become someone who struggles to open up emotionally, maintaining a façade of "*self-sufficiency*" that hides the fear of being vulnerable.

Over time, this behavioral pattern can lead us to live in isolation—not due to a lack of people around us, but due to our unwillingness to allow others to be part of our lives in a deeper and more genuine way. And that is when the defense mechanism that once protected us from pain turns into an obstacle to fully experiencing life.

Inflexibility

Inflexibility is a defense mechanism that arises when we perceive hidden rejection stemming from family instability. Often, we find ourselves in situations where our family goes through crises, conflicts, and unexpected changes. These experiences create an environment of uncertainty, where rules and behaviors become unpredictable. When this happens, we develop a need to keep everything under control and create rigid structures in our lives to avoid any form of emotional disorder.

From childhood, we may have experienced events that foster this inflexibility. For example, when our parents frequently argue or go through separations, we feel the need to find stability amid the chaos. In these moments, our minds may lead us to adopt rigid behaviors to protect ourselves from the emotional pain caused by family instability. As a result, we begin to fear change, as any alteration in our daily lives or family dynamics can be seen as a threat.

When we witness family instability—such as a lack of communication or constant conflicts—it teaches us to build walls around our emotions. Inflexibility can manifest in various areas of our lives, including personal and professional relationships, where we become reluctant to accept new ideas or approaches. For example, in a group of friends, we might insist on always choosing the same place to go out, fearing that a new experience could bring more chaos and disharmony.

If, during adolescence, we experience frequent relocations due to family financial struggles, we learn to value predictability and security. This pursuit of control can lead to an "*all or nothing*" mentality, where we believe that things must be done in one specific way and any deviation is unacceptable.

Our inflexible behavior can also manifest in the workplace. If, during our youth, we witnessed our parents facing job crises and constantly changing positions, we may internalize the idea that we need to be extremely strict with our performance, avoiding any possibility of error. This can lead us to reject constructive feedback or resist new methodologies, as they may be perceived as a threat to our sense of control.

Ultimately, this rigidity prevents us from adapting to new circumstances and genuinely connecting with others. Inflexibility, in the end, becomes a barrier that isolates us and hinders our emotional growth.

Pause to Reflect

- Do I feel the need to have complete control over everything around me in order to feel safe and at peace?
- Do I avoid situations where I cannot control the outcome, even when it means missing out on opportunities for personal or professional growth?
- Do I realize that my need to have things "*my way*" can create conflicts in my relationships, such as when I insist on controlling all the day-to-day decisions?
- Do I feel the need to do everything with excellence, leaving no room for mistakes?
- Do I avoid new or challenging situations out of fear of not being perfect?
- Do I notice that my pursuit of perfection prevents me from enjoying the process or celebrating my achievements?
- Do I feel the need to control small details of my daily life or environment to feel more secure?
- Do I tend to repeat certain actions, like a ritual, believing that this will ensure things don't spiral out of control?
- Do I realize that I have such rigid standards in various areas of my life that any deviation causes me anxiety?
- Do I feel that I must do everything alone to ensure things are done correctly?
- Do I hesitate to seek help or support because I fear others will see me as weak or incapable?
- Do I realize that my difficulty in opening up to others or sharing my vulnerabilities leaves me emotionally isolated?

- Am I reluctant to accept new ideas or changes in my daily life?
- How does my resistance to change affect my relationships?
- Do I recognize that my inflexibility has kept me from achieving my goals, even when change could be beneficial?

The Weight of Self-Sufficiency

When I reached my final year of college in Systems Analysis and Development, I landed my first job in the IT field at a mid-sized company. The department was officially called "IT" (Information Technology), but in practice, it meant being the infamous "jack of all trades." Have you ever heard that joke?

"What's your profession?"

"I'm a programmer."

"Oh, great! Can you fix my printer?"

Well, it's not really a joke. That's exactly how people—and worse, business owners—see the role of IT professionals.

I was hired to develop a new website for the company and create technological tools to optimize the marketing and sales departments. However, the reality was quite different: my role revolved around managing the network, fixing old computers, and, of course, dealing with problematic printers. Although my background was in analysis and development, I had basic knowledge of networking, servers, and maintenance, so I took on the challenge.

The company's network was a complete mess—entirely misconfigured, lacking security, and running on equipment that had survived a flood that had hit the office the previous year. But despite the technical challenges, the biggest obstacle I faced wasn't the infrastructure—it was the workplace environment.

The person who held the position before me had left due to terminal stomach cancer. He was practically a legend within the company—he had worked there his entire life, was highly respected, and had built the company's entire technological infrastructure. He knew every detail and quirk of the systems by heart, but then the flood destroyed nearly everything, coinciding with his departure.

As a newcomer and an unknown face, I inevitably became the target of comparisons. Any delay in solving a problem was met with comments like, "*So-and-so could do this with his eyes closed.*" People frequently suggested that I call him for help. Even though I knew, rationally, that this was the best course of action, my pride and sense of self-sufficiency made it difficult to reach out. But to avoid complaints, I ended up asking for his help, and he was always willing to assist—after all, no one knew that environment better than he did. A few months later, however, he passed away.

From that moment on, the pressure I felt increased dramatically. Without the possibility of relying on his expertise, my insecurity and fear of rejection became even more intense, fueling a growing need for absolute control and isolation in the face of challenges. Even when I faced problems that were clearly beyond my technical abilities, I took full responsibility, convinced that I had to handle everything on my own.

The situation reached its breaking point when the company's network was hacked by ransomware—a cyberattack in which hackers seize and encrypt data, demanding a ransom for its release. Despite my inexperience, I did everything in my power to safeguard the data and maintain network security. While I succeeded technically, the emotional toll was devastating—I felt like I was crumbling inside.

With each new problem, I could feel the weight of comparison in people's eyes. It drained my energy to the point that, one morning, while waiting for the bus to work, I felt as if I was having a heart attack—an unbearable pressure in my chest, numbness in my arms, and an overwhelming sense of dread. In that moment, I made a decision: as soon as I got to work, I would quit. I didn't care if I had to go hungry—I would not spend another day in that place.

I arrived at the company, walked straight into my manager's office, and, without hesitation, told her I wanted to leave. I explained how I felt and asked to leave immediately. Her response took me by surprise. She listened carefully and said:

" Gerson, why did you let it get to this point? Why didn't you tell us you needed help? We would have supported you. We like your work. Of course, the comparisons were always going to be there—the previous IT guy was a part of our history, he was practically family. But that doesn't mean we didn't appreciate what you were

doing. We had no idea you were under so much pressure. If you ever change your mind, our doors will always be open for you."

At the time, I heard her words, but I didn't truly absorb their meaning. My wounds of rejection were so overwhelming that, at the end of our conversation, I walked out of her office, grabbed my things, and left the company without saying goodbye to anyone. I never went back.

I wasn't aware of how The Hidden Wound of Rejection had influenced the entire situation. Today, after applying these reflection exercises, I see things much more clearly. I realize that many of my decisions were driven by my defense mechanisms. If I hadn't been so consumed by the need for validation—so fiercely self-sufficient—I would have asked for help, and the story might have turned out differently.

In the next chapter, we will explore behaviors that directly impact your ability to build and maintain relationships.

6

ABILITY TO RELATE

Relationships and social interactions are essential components of the human experience, shaping not only how we see ourselves but also how we perceive and connect with the world around us. When we develop wounds of rejection in our relationships, it deeply impacts the way we interact with others, making it difficult to build healthy and meaningful connections.

In this context, behaviors such as social anxiety, fear of intimacy, emotional dependency, conflict avoidance, the need for approval, and isolation become protective responses to hidden wounds of rejection. Throughout our lives, these responses may emerge as attempts to avoid the pain of rejection and the experience of feeling unworthy.

As we explore each of these behaviors, we will uncover how they intertwine with our personal experiences and the importance of recognizing them so that we can develop healthier and more fulfilling relationships.

Social Anxiety

Social anxiety is another defense mechanism that emerges when the hidden wound of rejection stems from experiences of public humiliation. Throughout our lives, we often find ourselves in situations where we are exposed to the critical gaze of others, and this exposure can trigger deep insecurity and a fear of being judged. When we become the target of laughter, criticism, or devaluation in social settings, that pain transforms into an overwhelming fear that leads us to avoid social interactions.

We recall moments when humiliation occurred in situations that, at first glance, might have seemed trivial but left a lasting impact on our psyche. For example, a school presentation where we forgot our lines and, instead of receiving support, were ridiculed by our peers. This experience not only imprinted the label of "*failure*" in our minds but also created the belief that being in public is synonymous with vulnerability and pain.

Another situation that comes to mind is when, during a team game, we made a mistake that cost the victory. Instead of receiving encouragement, we were met with harsh criticism and blame from teammates, turning that mistake into a source of shame. These episodes teach us that social interactions can be hostile environments, prompting our minds to seek ways to protect us, ultimately leading to the development of social anxiety.

We also remember instances where humiliation took place within our own families. A demeaning comment made by a relative during a family dinner—mocking an effort or an achievement—may have left a wound that refuses to heal. These experiences are not just memorable;

they shape our perception that the world is a place where vulnerability can be punished. As a result, we begin to avoid social situations for fear that history will repeat itself.

Thus, social anxiety becomes a shield we attempt to raise against the pain of exposure and rejection. The fear of judgment can lead us to avoid social events, parties, or even everyday interactions. However, this excessive protection isolates us, preventing us from experiencing the human connections we deeply desire, perpetuating a cycle of loneliness and insecurity.

Fear of Intimacy

Fear of intimacy is a defense mechanism that develops in response to the hidden wound of rejection caused by experiences of emotional abandonment. When we feel that we lack adequate emotional support—especially in childhood and adolescence—this fear takes root within us, affecting the way we relate to others. We are always seeking meaningful connections, yet we often feel insecure and reluctant to fully open up to someone. The fear of being vulnerable—and consequently being rejected—prevents us from experiencing healthy and fulfilling relationships.

Events that indicate a lack of emotional support shape our behavior toward intimacy. For example, we may have faced the absence of a parent who was not there to comfort or support us during crucial moments. This creates a deep feeling that we are not worthy of love or attention. Another example is when our emotional expressions were frequently ignored, leading us to believe that our feelings are not valid or that we do not deserve to be heard.

Fear of intimacy can also manifest during adolescence when we experience relationships in which trust is broken—whether through betrayals, secrets, or disappointments. When a close friend lets us down, we may shut ourselves off and avoid forming new friendships, fearing that the pain of betrayal will happen again. We also remember moments when we tried to share our feelings but were met with criticism or indifference, making us feel vulnerable and insecure.

These experiences lead us to build walls around ourselves, making it difficult to form deep and meaningful connections. We start to believe that by keeping ourselves emotionally distant, we can avoid the pain of rejection and abandonment. However, this defense strategy prevents us from experiencing the true intimacy and love that we long for.

Fear of intimacy is a self-perpetuating cycle, where our need for connection is constantly sabotaged by our own fears and insecurities.

Emotional Dependence

Emotional dependence is a defense mechanism we develop in response to the hidden wound of rejection that arise when a lack of affection becomes a constant in our lives. When we reflect on our experiences, we can identify significant moments of abandonment or emotional absence that have shaped our behavior. These episodes often occur in childhood and adolescence, forming the foundation of our need to seek affection and validation in future relationships.

We are shaped by the interactions we have with the people around us. For us, the absence of affection can manifest in different ways. We may recall moments when our parents or caregivers were physically present but emotionally distant, leaving us with the feeling that we were not important enough. The lack of hugs, words of encouragement, or moments of tenderness can create a deep void in our hearts, leading us to constantly seek approval and love from others.

For example, growing up in an environment where communication was scarce and emotions were frequently ignored teaches us that love is a rare currency. This perception may have taken root when one of us, seeking comfort, was discouraged by a family member from expressing emotions, leading to the belief that our feelings were not valid. Another example is a school friendship that suddenly ended without explanation, leaving us with a sense of abandonment and reinforcing the belief that we would never be truly worthy of love.

As we move into adolescence, these patterns may intensify. We may have witnessed romantic relationships where love seemed conditional, and our self-esteem became tied to how we were treated. We remember trying hard to please our partners, believing that this would secure their affection and attention. When these relationships ended, the pain of rejection became overwhelming, and the lack of affection left us with a deep longing to cling to anyone who showed even the slightest sign of care.

This pattern continues into adulthood, where emotional dependence can manifest in various ways. We may struggle with being alone, fearing the loneliness and rejection that come with it. Often, we cling to people who do not treat us well, believing that the scarcity of affection justifies the suffering. The need to always be with someone becomes a defense mechanism—a way to protect ourselves from the pain of the lack of love we experienced in childhood.

Conflict Avoidance

Conflict avoidance is a defense mechanism we develop when the hidden wound of rejection stems from family invalidation. When we feel ignored, criticized, or dismissed at home, we create strategies to avoid situations that might cause further tension. Instead of facing disagreements, expressing our opinions, or defending our boundaries, we choose to remain silent, submit, or withdraw. This gives us a false sense of peace and control, but in the long run, it fuels frustration, low self-esteem, and even resentment.

During childhood and adolescence, family invalidation can manifest in different ways. Perhaps our perspectives were never taken seriously, or our emotional needs were neglected. Growing up in an environment where our thoughts and feelings were constantly minimized or ridiculed can make us resistant to conflict, fearing further rejection or dismissal.

For example, imagine a child who, every time they try to express a different opinion from their parents, hears phrases like, "*You don't know what you're talking about,*" or "*Children shouldn't have an opinion.*" Over time, they learn that their thoughts have no value and begin to conform to what others say, even when it makes them uncomfortable. Another common scenario is growing up in a household with constant arguments. To avoid being an additional "*problem,*" we may choose to stay silent and never challenge anything, no matter how much we disagree. This behavior, shaped in childhood, carries over into adulthood.

When invalidation happens repeatedly over long periods, we may learn that any confrontation makes us vulnerable to rejection, leading us to withdraw from expressing ourselves authentically. We become "*peacemakers,*" avoiding arguments and disagreements at all costs—often at the expense of our own needs and desires. In interpersonal relationships, professional life, and even within our families, we choose silence and submission over facing conflict.

In situations like an important conversation with a boss, we may remain silent, accepting decisions that harm or overwhelm us instead of asserting our position. In friendships or romantic relationships, we avoid confronting behaviors that hurt or upset us, fearing that doing so might jeopardize the relationship or cause discomfort.

Conflict avoidance is a shield we build to protect ourselves from rejection, but it also becomes a prison that prevents us from forming authentic and healthy relationships. After all, conflict is not necessarily destructive;

when handled in a healthy way, it allows us to grow, communicate, and set clear boundaries. However, when family invalidation shapes our perception from an early age, we come to believe that conflict only brings more pain, leading us to suppress ourselves rather than stand our ground.

Once we realize that our fear of conflict does not protect us but instead isolates us from our true voice, we can begin to build more balanced relationships and reclaim the value that was denied to us during childhood.

Examples of family invalidation that lead to conflict avoidance:

- Being constantly interrupted or ignored during family conversations, leading the child to believe their opinions don't matter.
- Having emotions minimized or ridiculed by parents, such as when a child expresses sadness or anger and hears responses like, "*That's silly, you're overreacting.*"
- Growing up in an environment where only the authority figure's opinion matters, such as in households where one parent always has the final say, leaving no room for questioning.
- Being compared unfavorably to siblings or peers, creating the feeling that any attempt to stand out or assert boundaries will be met with criticism and invalidation.

These experiences shape our behavior throughout life, causing us to adopt conflict avoidance as a defense mechanism against the pain of rejection.

The Need for Approval

This behavioral pattern emerges when we have been exposed to experiences of social exclusion that left a deep mark on us. The fear of being excluded, of not belonging, or of being seen as different or inadequate by our peers shapes the way we act and relate to others. As a result, we develop a constant need to seek external approval as a way to compensate for the wound of rejection experienced in the past.

As children, the desire to be accepted is natural. We need affection, acceptance, and a sense of belonging, both within our families and in social settings. However, when this belonging is denied, a deep fear of rejection takes root. Consequently, the habit of seeking approval begins to form as a defense mechanism. We adjust to what we believe others expect from us, minimizing or even hiding our true opinions, feelings, and desires to avoid the risk of being rejected again.

Social Exclusion and the Need for Approval

In childhood, moments of social exclusion can be devastating. For example:

- At school, we may have been left out of friend groups, not invited to parties, or even bullied, making us feel that we had to "*earn*" others' acceptance.
- Within the family, constant comparisons between siblings or cousins—where one is always praised while the other is ignored or criticized—can create an ongoing effort to please and be recognized, in hopes of finally receiving the approval that was denied.
- In extracurricular activities, such as sports or clubs, exclusion can occur when we are not chosen for teams or groups, leading us to believe we are "*not good enough*" and must work harder to be accepted.
- Among childhood or teenage friends, we may have been ignored or dismissed for our tastes, appearance, or behaviors that were considered "*outside the norm.*" This kind of exclusion can create a need to shape our personality to fit others' standards.

These moments of rejection—especially during childhood and adolescence, which are crucial periods for identity development—become deeply ingrained in our subconscious. As a defense mechanism, we begin to base our decisions and behaviors on pleasing others, constantly seeking signs that we are accepted and valued.

Consequences of the Need for Approval

Over time, this need for approval becomes a burden. We struggle to act authentically because we are always afraid of how others will react. Our decisions become driven by what we think others will approve of, rather than what we truly want. This behavior can negatively impact multiple areas of life:

- In personal relationships, we may suppress our true selves, avoiding disagreements with partners or friends out of fear of criticism or abandonment.
- At work, we might find it difficult to say "*no*", taking on more responsibilities than we can handle just to please bosses or colleagues.
- In social interactions, we may shape our tastes, opinions, and behaviors to align with the group instead of expressing our true personality.
- Within the family, we may continuously seek validation from parents or other family members, even as adults, in an attempt to finally receive the recognition we always felt was missing.

The need for approval is exhausting because it keeps us in a constant state of alert, searching for signs of acceptance and constantly adjusting our behavior to please others. It prevents us from being authentic, keeping us trapped in the fear that we are never good enough.

Isolation

Isolation is another emotional defense mechanism that develops when we are repeatedly excluded or undervalued by groups—whether at school, within the family, or in social circles. When the hidden wound of rejection takes deep root, our natural reaction is to protect ourselves by withdrawing. This leads us to believe that by keeping our distance, we can avoid the pain and suffering of being rejected again.

We may recall childhood situations where we were systematically excluded by classmates. Whether due to not fitting certain standards—such as clothing, behavior, or even interests—this rejection manifests in many ways: being the last to be chosen for a team, not being invited to events or parties, or being the target of constant jokes.

Within the family environment, isolation can also be a response to the persistent feeling of being undervalued. Some of us grew up in households where our interests, emotions, or talents were ignored or ridiculed by other family members. Perhaps a sibling was always favored, or our parents constantly compared our achievements to those of others. This can lead us to believe that no matter what we do, we will never be accepted or valued. To escape this painful cycle, we withdraw emotionally and physically, isolating ourselves even from those who should offer us unconditional support.

During adolescence, the desire to be part of a group becomes even stronger. Many of us have experienced the pain of not being accepted into certain social circles. We may have been rejected for not fitting specific behavioral or appearance standards or simply for having different opinions.

In adulthood, isolation can also manifest in the workplace. Experiences of exclusion—such as being ignored in meetings, not being included in important decisions, or not receiving proper recognition for our efforts—reinforce the feeling that we do not belong.

Isolation is neither a natural nor a desirable state but rather a defense mechanism we construct to protect ourselves from the pain of rejection. Unfortunately, by withdrawing, we also miss the opportunity to build meaningful connections that could help heal the wounds left by rejection. Understanding that isolation is a response to continuous rejection gives us the chance to question and challenge this behavior, allowing us to gradually open ourselves to social interaction once again.

Pause to Reflect

- When I receive invitations to events, do I feel a mix of wanting to participate and fearing rejection, which causes great discomfort?
- In meetings or presentations, does the anticipation of being judged or making mistakes paralyze me, affecting my self-confidence?
- In casual encounters, do I become so focused on how I will be perceived that I often lose my naturalness in interactions?
- In difficult moments, do I hesitate to share my feelings, fearing that it might change how others see me?
- Do deep discussions make me uncomfortable, and do I feel an urge to shift the focus to neutral topics?
- Do I tend to maintain emotional barriers as a way to avoid possible disappointments or rejections?

- After bad experiences, is my default response to distance myself from intimate relationships and keep everything at a superficial level?
- Do I feel anxious when I notice that a friendship or relationship is changing, preferring to withdraw before being abandoned?
- Do small signs of distancing from others make me act defensively, often reinforcing the separation even further?
- Does the idea of spending time alone make me restless, and do I frequently seek external distractions to fill this void?
- Do I prefer activities that involve other people, even when they are unnecessary, because I fear the feeling of isolation?
- Do I often put others' needs before my own, even knowing it could harm me?
- Do I avoid saying "*no*" and tend to give in to others' desires out of fear of disappointing them or being seen as selfish?
- Do I rely on external approval to make important decisions or feel secure in my choices?
- Do everyday activities, like posting on social media or sharing achievements, often come with a need for external validation?
- Do I often avoid disagreeing or suggesting different ideas to prevent misunderstandings?
- At work and in relationships, do I accept decisions I don't fully agree with to maintain harmony?

- Do I tend to wait for conflicts to resolve themselves, avoiding discussions or uncomfortable conversations?
- Do I overlook harmful behaviors in others, believing that time will fix the situation?
- When thinking about saying "*no*" or setting boundaries, do I feel a mix of guilt and fear of rejection?
- Do I often prioritize others' well-being over my own, fearing that my stance might be misinterpreted or criticized?
- Do small social interactions make me anxious because I fear not meeting the expectations of those around me?
- Do I constantly look for ways to please others, even if it goes against my own desires or values?
- At events or in interactions, do I adapt my behavior to align with what I believe the group will accept?
- Do I choose paths that bring social approval, even when they don't represent what I truly want?
- Do I take on more responsibilities than I can handle out of fear of disappointing others?
- In relationships, do I accept uncomfortable situations to avoid confrontation or criticism?
- Do I avoid expressing my ideas or opening up emotionally in groups to minimize the risk of rejection?
- Do I often feel that others can't understand my feelings or point of view, which makes me prefer isolation?
- Do I try to avoid forming new social connections, believing that no one would truly care about what I have to say?

- Does distancing myself from people seem like a safe way to avoid possible rejection or judgment?
- Do internal conflicts often lead me to choose isolation as a form of self-protection?

Silent Anguish

At the end of eighth grade, I asked my father if I could move in with him. On the eve of my move to his house, I made a decision that makes me reflect even today. I got rid of my entire collection of cassette tapes filled with national and international pop rock music that I loved so much. Why? Because I believed that he, as someone who appeared to listen only to classical music, would not accept me if he knew about my musical tastes. So, I started listening to Mozart, Beethoven, Bach, Tchaikovsky, Schubert, Chopin, Vivaldi, Wagner, and others. Not out of passion, but purely as an attempt to belong.

During the time I lived with him, I felt no effort on his part to ease my need for acceptance or my wound of rejection. On the contrary, living with someone who was so erudite but completely incapable of expressing emotions or creating space for vulnerability only intensified my defense mechanisms. Today, looking back, I recall some behaviors that leave me perplexed... or perhaps I don't even want to think too much about them.

We lived in one city, and I studied in another. My father would give me money for transportation and lunch. Sometimes, he gave enough for two days; other times, for the whole week. Occasionally, I would catch a ride with him, but most of the time, I took the bus. And this is where my anguish revealed itself in a way that was almost comical yet deeply telling.

When the money ran out, asking for more was a real internal battle. My avoidance of conflict—even when, in this case, the conflict didn't actually exist—was so intense that I would postpone the request until the last possible moment. The feeling was agonizing, like a weight growing heavier by the minute, until I had no choice but to speak. If I was taking the bus, I would wait until the very moment I had to leave the house to ask. Many times, I even woke him up to ask for the money because I couldn't bring myself to ask the night before, before we went to bed. If I was getting a ride, I would wait until the exact moment I was stepping out of the car. The drop-off point was in a very busy area where stopping was difficult. He always took advantage of a red light so that I could get out quickly. And at that precise moment, with him already looking ahead, about to drive off, I would blurt out: "*Dad, I need money.*" Choosing that moment made everything even more awkward and reinforced my sense of inadequacy. This scene repeated itself countless times during the years I lived with him. Today, when I think back on this behavior, I realize how much the hidden wound of rejection shaped my choices and decisions.

As you can see, the hidden wound of rejection has a profound impact on our ability to relate to others. And since we are constantly forming relationships, it's easy to imagine the damage this feeling can cause in our lives. This set of behaviors highlights how hidden rejection places us in a kind of parallel reality, shaping a life completely different from what it could be if this emotional wound were not so exposed.

I hope you have dedicated yourself to the reflection exercises proposed so far and that, with each chapter, you are diving deeper into your journey of self-discovery. Now, let's explore the set of behaviors associated with the "*routine*" of procrastination and performance, and understand how these defense mechanisms can influence and shape our lives.

7

PROCRASTINATION AND PERFORMANCE

Procrastination and performance are two deeply interconnected aspects of an individual's life. What we often perceive as mere "*laziness*" or "*lack of motivation*" may, in reality, conceal the influence of the hidden wound of rejection. It directly affects how we handle tasks, responsibilities, and challenges.

In the realm of procrastination and performance, the wound of rejection acts as a silent barrier, generating insecurity, fear, and self-sabotage. The need for external validation, the constant fear of failure, or personal devaluation can trigger behaviors that negatively impact our ability to achieve our goals. Here, the hidden wound of rejection manifests itself as patterns of procrastination, premature abandonment, and the underutilization of our true potential.

This set of behaviors is linked to our relationship with work, studies, personal projects, and ambitions. It reflects how the fear of failure or lack of recognition can make us postpone decisions, abandon efforts, or even sabotage ourselves in the face of great opportunities. Each behavior within this group carries its own dynamic, always rooted in a hidden wound of rejection formed at some point. This wound manifests as a constant echo, paralyzing us and preventing us from moving forward with confidence.

Now, we will explore how these behaviors—chronic procrastination, premature abandonment, underutilization of potential, fear of failure, and self-sabotage—are formed. We will see how experiences of lack of validation, academic devaluation, or excessive expectations may have contributed to the development of these defense mechanisms, affecting not only our productivity but also our self-esteem and vision of the future.

By understanding the impact of the wound of rejection on performance, we can begin to dismantle these barriers and work toward a more productive and balanced life, with less self-criticism and more compassion for ourselves.

Chronic Procrastination

Chronic procrastination is the persistent tendency to postpone important tasks, even when we know it may lead to negative consequences. While it may seem like a simple issue of poor time management or lack of discipline, chronic procrastination is often deeply tied to an emotional defense mechanism. It arises when the wound of rejection, stemming from a lack of validation, shapes our attitudes toward work, responsibilities, and even our own dreams.

When our achievements or efforts are not acknowledged—or worse, are constantly criticized or minimized—we begin to associate completing tasks with potential rejection. If, in childhood, we were often ignored when trying to show something we created, or if we never received praise for our efforts, we internalized the belief that our work, our ideas, and even we ourselves are unworthy of recognition. Procrastination then becomes a way to avoid this feeling of invalidation—an unconscious attempt to protect ourselves from yet another experience of rejection.

Why give our best if, in the end, the result will likely be ignored or criticized? Why put in the effort if validation and recognition will never come? These questions, though not always conscious, echo in our minds, making it difficult to start or continue tasks that require commitment and effort.

Examples of Lack of Validation

As children, we may have spent hours carefully drawing a picture, only to hear a quick, unenthusiastic comment from someone we hoped to impress, like, "*Oh, that's nice.*" Or, after bringing home good grades, we were compared to a sibling or friend who always did better, making our own successes feel small and insignificant.

As teenagers, we may have worked hard on a school project or extracurricular activity, only to be ignored while the more popular students received all the attention. Perhaps, when sharing our ideas and ambitions with someone we trusted, we didn't receive the encouragement we had hoped for, leading us to question the value of our own opinions—and, ultimately, our own worth.

These moments of invalidation create the perception that our efforts are not worthwhile because recognition will never come. Over time, procrastination emerges as a defense mechanism to protect us from the pain of rejection. By delaying action, we avoid the risk of exposing our flaws and vulnerabilities to others' opinions, keeping ourselves safe within a comfort zone. However, this mechanism distances us from new opportunities for growth and development, creating a vicious cycle in which the fear of not being validated prevents us from taking action, and the lack of action perpetuates the absence of recognition.

However, when we identify and understand that this behavior is actually a response to a lack of emotional validation, we can begin to challenge this pattern. Procrastinating does not protect us from future rejection; it only prevents us from revealing our true potential. To break this cycle, we must recognize the intrinsic value of our efforts, regardless of external validation.

Chronic procrastination has deep roots in how we see ourselves and how we have been seen by others throughout our lives. Acknowledging this connection allows us not only to address the behavior itself but also to heal the emotional wounds at its core.

Premature Abandonment

Premature abandonment is a common trap for many of us. It is a defense mechanism rooted in the hidden wound of rejection, developed through repeated experiences of failure. This behavior is triggered when, over the course of our lives, we accumulate experiences in which we attempted to achieve something but, for various reasons, were unable to succeed. In response to these failures, our brain develops a self-protection strategy: giving up too soon to avoid the emotional distress of yet another defeat. Instead of persisting, we shield ourselves from the emotional exhaustion that failures can cause.

We can observe how premature abandonment is shaped by repeated failures experienced in childhood and adolescence. When we are repeatedly exposed to situations where our efforts do not yield success, we begin to form the belief that continuing to try is futile. These failures can manifest in many ways: in academics, sports, interpersonal relationships, and even family dynamics.

Repeated Failures and Premature Abandonment

Consider, for example, a child who consistently puts effort into learning something new at school but, for whatever reason, continues to receive low grades. They may begin to believe that no matter how much they study, the result will never be satisfactory. Over time, this child develops a tendency to avoid new academic challenges and, instead of persevering, chooses to give up at the very beginning of a new task. The feeling that their failures are proof of incompetence takes root, and the fear of repeating this cycle of failure becomes paralyzing.

Another example can be seen in sports. A child who repeatedly finishes last in competitions or is never chosen for the main team may begin to internalize the idea that they are not good enough. They may even enjoy the activity, but the fear of failing again and again leads them to quit before they have a chance to improve their skills. The result? A cycle of self-sabotage in which they avoid situations where, with more practice and time, they could have achieved good results.

In the family context, we can observe situations where a child tries to please their parents or gain approval in different areas of life but never seems to meet their expectations. This repeated failure to gain recognition can lead to an attitude of abandonment, where they stop trying to impress or seek family approval, instead choosing emotional isolation.

This type of defensive behavior is especially common when rejection associated with repeated failures is experienced from an early age. For many of us, this defense mechanism continues to operate into adulthood, limiting our achievements in different areas of life.

Underutilization of Potential

When we reflect on our lives, it is hard not to notice how much of our potential remains unexplored. Underutilization of potential is not merely a matter of lacking effort; it originates when the hidden wound of rejection stems from experiences of academic devaluation during childhood and adolescence. It is as if, due to certain events, we decide to hide, choosing not to stand out and not to actively pursue what we are truly capable of achieving.

All of us have faced situations that made us feel undervalued. These experiences may have come from different sources: teachers, peers, or even family members. Moments when a teacher, instead of encouraging us, made deprecating comments about our performance, highlighting our mistakes rather than recognizing our efforts. These episodes not only undermined our confidence but also planted the idea that we were not good enough. This devaluation can be devastating, especially during formative years when external validation plays a crucial role in shaping our self-image and motivation.

Examples of Academic Devaluation

- When presenting a school project, a teacher said the work was not good enough, suggesting that we lacked talent. This criticism was internalized, and since then, we have avoided engaging in activities that require creativity or public presentations.
- In the classroom, a peer always stood out and received praise, while we were often ignored. This constant comparison made us feel that our efforts were in vain, leading us to settle for mediocrity and stop seeking to develop our own potential.
- We grew up in households where academic success was seen as trivial. When we received high grades, praise was rare, but any mistake or low score became a topic of discussion. This led us to believe that our achievements did not matter, making us hesitant to take on more complex challenges.
- While working on a group project, our ideas were disregarded and replaced by suggestions from others.

This created a sense of powerlessness, leading us to avoid contributing in future collaborations, preferring to stay in the background rather than risk being rejected again.

Underutilization of potential, as a result of academic devaluation, is a defense mechanism that prevents us from fully exploring our capabilities. Instead of seeking new challenges and opportunities, we often settle for what is safe and familiar, allowing our true essence to remain hidden. However, by understanding that these experiences do not define who we are, we can begin to work toward unlocking our potential and achieving our true aspirations.

Fear of Failure and Self-Sabotage

The fear of failure and self-sabotage are deeply interconnected, forming a cycle that limits our personal and professional growth. Both are defense mechanisms born from the wound of rejection, triggered by high expectations, and manifest as emotional barriers that prevent us from moving forward.

The Weight of Expectations

From childhood, we are bombarded with expectations, whether explicit or implicit. It could be a father who expects you to be the best student in class or a mother who dreams of you becoming a great athlete. While these expectations may seem motivating, they often turn into unbearable burdens. A classic example is the insistence on achieving high grades in school, with the promise that academic success will guarantee a bright future. This constant pressure creates anxiety and fuels the fear of failure, making you believe that any mistake or underperformance will be catastrophic.

During adolescence, this dynamic intensifies. Participating in extracurricular activities such as sports tournaments or theater performances can bring a mix of excitement and fear. The desire to meet others' expectations often outweighs the willingness to enjoy the experience, leading you to avoid challenges that could foster growth. The idea of not living up to expectations becomes so paralyzing that giving up feels safer than risking failure.

Over time, this fear of failure evolves into self-sabotaging behaviors. When you avoid challenging situations or procrastinate on important tasks, you are, in reality, trying to protect your most vulnerable self from the pain of rejection. Thus, when faced with situations that could expose flaws—such as taking on a difficult project at work or striving for a promotion—you prefer not to try, convinced that failure would be devastating.

Self-sabotage also manifests in constant comparison with others. As a teenager, upon noticing that peers seemed more successful, you may have withdrawn, avoiding exposing your vulnerabilities. This pattern often persists into adulthood, where the fear of rejection or criticism leads you to avoid new friendships, opportunities, or professional challenges.

This behavior not only limits your growth but also reinforces a sense of inadequacy, creating a difficult cycle to break. Additionally, the pressure for perfection and the constant pursuit of others' approval directly impact your emotional well-being.

Recognizing that both fear of failure and self-sabotage have roots in past experiences—often shaped by unrealistic expectations—is the first step toward overcoming them.

Pause to Reflect

- Do I postpone work or study projects out of fear that my effort won't be valued?
- Do I avoid committing to long-term goals because I need constant validation?
- Do I delay important decisions for fear of criticism or disapproval?
- Do I avoid changes, such as switching jobs or moving to a new city, because I fear not receiving support?
- Do I procrastinate starting businesses or projects out of fear of criticism?
- Do I abandon projects or activities before fully dedicating myself, or because I lack support?
- Do I start something with enthusiasm but lose motivation when I don't see quick results?
- Does my fear of failure prevent me from committing to new opportunities?
- Do I hesitate to change careers or start a business because I fear not succeeding?
- Do I feel discouraged after unsuccessful attempts?
- Do I avoid making new friends or starting creative projects due to past experiences of rejection?

- Have I avoided applying for jobs or sharing ideas out of fear of being judged?
- Have I refused to lead or contribute to projects, believing my skills were inadequate?
- Do I let negative opinions influence my choices?
- Have I avoided public speaking or pursuing opportunities after receiving criticism from colleagues or supervisors?
- Have I given up on courses or hobbies due to discouraging comments from others?
- Do I postpone projects or changes because I don't feel prepared or capable of succeeding?
- Do I criticize myself when I make mistakes and avoid trying again?
- When receiving constructive criticism, do I give up on new challenges because I feel incapable?
- Do I procrastinate on important tasks, even knowing it could harm me?
- Do I delay taking care of my health because I fear failing to maintain the commitment?

Unrealized Potential

Throughout my life, I have embraced an entrepreneurial and creative mindset. I have imagined, dreamed, and planned countless projects. A few made it past the planning stage, but they were quickly abandoned. When I was an English teacher, I opened my own language course, only to shut it down in less than a month. Later, when I started working as a web designer and graphic designer, I founded my own advertising agency. Although it didn't close immediately, it also didn't survive long enough to become successful.

When I moved to a tourist town, I opened a snack bar, but it shut down after just three months. I created and planned numerous digital projects, but many never even saw the light of day. It was only after applying the techniques presented in this book that I came to understand the root causes behind these premature abandonments and the procrastination that had so often taken control of my life.

The origins of these behaviors trace back to significant moments in my teenage years. In seventh grade, I received a pamphlet from the Air Force. I was fascinated by everything I read and started dreaming about the possibility of joining the Air Force. I decided to write a letter to my father, expressing my desire and asking to enroll in the preparatory course. A few days later, he came to my grandmother's house. With a well-crafted speech, he presented every possible objection—from the extreme difficulty of passing the selection exam to the strict discipline required of an Air Force officer.

My constant need for approval left no room for questioning. Without hesitation, I abandoned that dream.

Years later, while living with him, I faced another pivotal moment. I was in my second year of high school, a time when we start thinking about college and the future. I felt deeply drawn to psychology and wanted to pursue it as a career. However, when I shared my plan, I was met with a resounding "*no*." My father wanted me to study law so that I could continue his work. He even claimed that if I chose psychology, I would end up "*starving to death.*" He added with irony, "*Who's going to pay just to sit and talk with a psychologist?*"

Once again, my need for approval took over. But this time, the fear of failure also came into play. What would happen if I defied my father, applied to a psychology program, and didn't get accepted? That possibility felt unbearable. So, I gave up on my desire, allowing doubt and fear to limit me.

From that moment on, I began to underutilize my potential. I lost interest in college altogether. I left home and became an English teacher in another city.

Next, we will explore the next set of behaviors: emotional reactivity.

8

EMOTIONAL REACTIVITY

Emotional reactivity refers to the intensity with which we respond emotionally to events or stimuli in our daily lives. When we talk about excessive reactivity, emotional outbursts, or uncontrolled anger, we are referring to a set of behaviors that reflect difficulty in regulating emotions in a healthy way. This pattern of behavior is directly linked to the wound of rejection, often stemming from repeated criticism, abandonment, negative comparisons, or frequent conflicts.

We all experience moments when our emotions feel overwhelming, but when these episodes become constant, it suggests the existence of automatic "*routines.*" These routines develop as defense mechanisms in response to rejections that marked our childhood and adolescence. The intensity of these emotional responses may vary, but what they all have in common is that, behind the exaggerated reactions, there is an attempt to protect ourselves from the pain of rejection.

Situations of rejection—such as harsh criticism, emotional abandonment, constant devaluation, or comparisons that make us feel inferior—can shape us to react disproportionately when we sense that these wounds are being reopened. As a result, emotional reactivity becomes a barrier to personal growth and healthy relationships, as we struggle to handle wounds of rejection in a balanced way.

Learning to regulate these emotions is essential to breaking the cycle of reactivity. By addressing each of the behaviors that contribute to emotional reactivity—such as excessive sensitivity, emotional dysregulation, defensiveness, constant irritability, and outbursts of anger—we can understand how these mechanisms emerged and, more importantly, how to overcome them. After all, emotional regulation is the key to building healthier relationships and living a more balanced life.

Excessive Reactivity

Excessive reactivity is a behavioral pattern we all recognize, even if we don't always identify it clearly. Often, we react disproportionately to comments or situations that, at first glance, seem harmless. These intense reactions are a form of defense—an emotional shield we raise when we feel our self-esteem is under attack. But why do we react this way? What makes us explode or shut down in response to something that, rationally, shouldn't affect us so deeply?

Excessive reactivity is a defense mechanism developed when the wound of rejection stems from harsh criticism. From an early age, we are sensitive to how others evaluate us, especially authority figures such as parents, teachers, or family members. When these criticisms are aggressive, harsh, or even humiliating, our natural response is to protect ourselves. Thus, we create an emotional barrier that manifests through exaggerated reactions.

During childhood and adolescence, we are particularly vulnerable to these criticisms. Imagine a child who, while trying to learn something new, constantly hears comments like, "*You never do anything right*" or "*Stop being useless!*" Over time, these aggressive remarks not only erode the child's confidence in their abilities but also plant the seed of reactivity. Whenever that person encounters a situation that reminds them of those early criticisms, they react intensely, as if they are being attacked all over again.

In adolescence, harsh criticism may come from classmates or authority figures, such as teachers who, instead of offering support, discourage with phrases like, "*You'll never pass this class.*" This kind of repeated rejection triggers a deep sense of inadequacy, making excessive reactivity an automatic response to avoid facing painful memories.

In adulthood, this behavior persists. We may react poorly to criticism at work, perceive threats in constructive feedback, or struggle in personal relationships when a partner or friend points out something that needs improvement. Our exaggerated reaction is not about what was said in the present—it's about the old wounds that past criticisms awaken in us.

Excessive reactivity, therefore, is a protective mechanism our brain developed to avoid reliving the rejection caused by past criticisms. However, instead of protecting us, this behavior prevents us from growing and listening to what could genuinely help us improve. It becomes a vicious cycle: we overreact to defend ourselves, but in doing so, we push away people and opportunities that could help us handle our emotions in a healthier way.

By understanding that our excessive reactivity is linked to a hidden wound of rejection rooted in childhood and adolescence, we can begin working on ways to regulate our emotions. We can learn to recognize when we are reacting disproportionately and find new ways to deal with discomfort. After all, the key to overcoming excessive reactivity lies in recognizing that, today, we are capable of handling criticism differently—with greater confidence and balance.

Emotional Dysregulation

Emotional dysregulation is a defense mechanism we develop when the hidden wound of rejection stems from abandonment. When we feel left behind—not just physically, but emotionally—the fear of being abandoned again can take over and cause us to lose control of our emotions.

We talk about emotional dysregulation when we encounter situations where we cannot regulate our reactions. These are sudden outbursts of anger, overwhelming sadness, or even deep despair that seem disproportionate to the triggering event. However, in reality, these episodes are tied to the pain caused by past experiences of feeling abandoned, alone, or neglected.

Abandonment can take many forms in childhood. It may be the distancing of a parental figure, an abrupt separation, or even the sense that our emotional needs were not consistently met. These experiences create deep insecurity, making us, as adults, prone to extreme reactions at the slightest sign of possible rejection or disconnection. Our emotional system, which should serve as a guide for self-regulation, instead becomes a trap that amplifies our responses to these triggers.

Examples of Abandonment Experienced in Childhood or Adolescence

- A parent left the family during childhood. Even if the separation was not physical or permanent, the emotional absence was felt. The fear that the people we love will leave us lingers, and at the slightest sign of someone pulling away, we react explosively.
- A sudden change of school or city disrupted all our friendships and connections without our control. This experience of loss can create the belief that people do not stay, leading to extreme emotional reactions whenever we sense a similar situation approaching.
- Growing up in an environment where our emotions were invalidated. If, whenever we felt sad or afraid, we were ignored or criticized for being "*weak,*" we learned to suppress our emotions. This kind of emotional abandonment causes feelings to accumulate until they eventually explode uncontrollably when we feel vulnerable.
- Losing an important figure without emotional support. Whether through the death of a beloved grandparent or the separation from a caregiver, if we lacked

proper explanations or emotional support to process grief, these unresolved experiences turn our emotions into a roller coaster whenever we face loss or separation.

Emotional dysregulation is a desperate attempt to avoid reliving these painful experiences. When we feel that someone might abandon us or that we are not being seen or heard, our brain goes into high alert. Emotions intensify, and instead of processing them calmly, we are overwhelmed by a flood of feelings we cannot contain.

In personal and professional relationships, this can be extremely damaging. We may find ourselves reacting with anger to situations that seem trivial to others. Or we may become paralyzed by sadness at moments that require clear thinking. These outbursts and moments of extreme vulnerability reflect a deep-seated fear of being left behind, rejected, or forgotten.

However, while emotional dysregulation is a natural defense response, it also prevents us from genuinely connecting with others and handling our feelings in a healthy way. We need to understand that the abandonment we fear is often more rooted in the past than in the present. When we start to recognize this, we can take the first steps toward healing and emotional resilience.

Defensive Behavior

Defensive behavior is an automatic reaction we develop when the hidden wound of rejection arise from feeling undervalued. Instead of opening ourselves up to constructive criticism or feedback that could help us grow, we shut down, erecting barriers and justifying our actions to avoid any sense of inadequacy. This behavior can isolate us and hinder our growth in various areas of life.

We all deal with harsh criticism or a lack of recognition for our qualities and achievements. When, in childhood or adolescence, we consistently feel undervalued by important figures in our lives, we internalize this devaluation as a personal threat. As a result, we begin reacting defensively whenever we sense this threat, even in situations where criticism is mild or constructive.

The Origins of Defensive Behavior

Let's reflect on some common experiences of devaluation in childhood or adolescence that can shape this behavior:

- Growing up in an environment where parents constantly pointed out mistakes without balancing them with praise or recognition of successes. For example, if we got a high grade in school but they only commented on the single point we missed, or if we did something well but they disregarded the effort and pointed out a minor flaw, this devaluation leaves an emotional imprint.

- Being compared to siblings, classmates, or other children from an early age. Phrases like "*Your brother got better grades*" or "*Why can't you be more like so-and-so?*" create a deep sense of inferiority and devaluation.
- Dedicating ourselves fully to a school activity or sport but never receiving the expected recognition. If teachers or coaches only focus on what we need to improve without acknowledging our efforts, this constant devaluation creates a defense mechanism. As adults, when facing evaluation or criticism, we react defensively to avoid feelings of failure or inadequacy.
- Experiencing ridicule or exclusion during childhood or adolescence also fuels defensive behavior. Children who experience bullying or rejection from peers often withdraw emotionally. For them, any comment or action reminiscent of past devaluation can trigger an immediate defensive reaction as a way to avoid reliving that emotional pain.

As adults, we continue carrying this emotional "*routine*" designed to protect us from devaluation. When we receive feedback at work, for example, we might react by justifying our actions or becoming defensive instead of absorbing the criticism constructively. In relationships, we may overreact to a partner's comment, interpreting it as an attack on our competence or worth, when in reality, it might just be a suggestion or a different perspective.

By shutting ourselves off from criticism, we miss valuable opportunities for learning and transformation. Defensive behavior, which seems like a short-term solution, ultimately traps us in a cycle of stagnation.

Constant Irritability

Constant irritability is a defense mechanism we develop when the hidden wound of rejection is triggered by negative comparisons. Growing up in environments where we are constantly compared to others—whether in performance, personality, or abilities—leads us to internalize the idea that we are never "*good enough*." This sense of inadequacy, fueled by repeated comparisons, can transform into constant irritation—a way to shield our self-esteem from further wounds.

When comparisons are repeated during vulnerable moments, their impact can be devastating. They create the belief that, no matter what we do, there will always be someone better, more talented, or more valued. Over time, the accumulation of these perceptions wears down our patience, making us react explosively to even the smallest comments. Thus, irritability becomes a defense mechanism, shielding an already wounded ego from further criticism.

The Impact of Comparisons in Childhood and Adolescence

During childhood, we are especially vulnerable to how others perceive and treat us. If we grow up in an environment where we are frequently compared to siblings, classmates, or other figures, it plants the seeds of constant irritability. These comparisons, which may seem harmless to those making them, deeply shape how we see ourselves.

In adolescence, when we seek affirmation and validation, this dynamic intensifies. Instead of receiving support, if we experience criticism disguised as comparison, we start preparing emotionally for an attack, reacting more aggressively and defensively.

Imagine a child who constantly hears from their parents that "*your older brother was always more studious*" or "*your cousin always got better grades.*" This child begins to associate their identity with a sense of inferiority. Over time, these repeated comparisons erode their self-confidence. As an adult, any criticism—no matter how mild—reopens this old wound, triggering an exaggerated response of irritation.

Negative Comparisons and Their Effects

- Academic Pressure: Being compared to classmates who achieve higher grades or possess specific skills can make a child feel less capable. If this pattern continues, they may carry this frustration into adulthood, reacting with irritability in situations involving evaluation or expectations.
- Sibling Rivalry: Growing up hearing that other siblings or cousins are "*more responsible,*" "*smarter,*" or "*more successful*" creates fertile ground for constant irritability. This can lead to a lifelong feeling of competition, leaving the person perpetually frustrated and impatient with criticism.
- Social Circles: Being compared to a more extroverted or popular friend can instill a deep sense of inferiority. Over time, this turns simple social interactions into

moments of tension, where any remark may be perceived as a veiled criticism.

- Workplace Dynamics: Repeatedly being compared to more successful or recognized colleagues can lead an individual to view all feedback as a threat. Irritability then manifests because every interaction with supervisors or coworkers reactivates the fear of not measuring up.

The Cycle of Irritability and Comparisons

This cycle of constant irritability can persist for years until it becomes embedded in our personality. Not only do we become more sensitive to direct comparisons, but we also start perceiving comparisons where they don't exist. A compliment given to someone else, a comment about how a colleague did something exceptionally well—these can all feel like subtle attacks on our worth.

Irritability, therefore, becomes a defense mechanism—a way to protect a self-esteem that has been wounded too many times in the past. But constant irritability is not just an exaggerated emotional response; it is a silent cry of pain, a reaction to the deep-seated fear of not being good enough.

By becoming aware of this mechanism, we can start to deconstruct this emotional pattern and gradually learn to handle our emotions and perceived criticisms in a healthier way.

Outbursts of Anger

Outbursts of anger are often a reflection of an emotional defense mechanism that we build when the wound of rejection originates from being exposed to frequent conflicts in our homes, social environments, or schools. Living in a context where conflicts are constant and intense weakens our ability to react in a balanced and controlled manner. As a result, we develop anger as a self-protection mechanism, a way to avoid or confront situations that make us relive the emotional pain of rejection.

In environments where conflicts are recurrent—whether it's family arguments, tensions between parents, or constant disputes with authority figures—our brain learns to anticipate confrontation. It prepares for defense, and often, this preparation manifests as emotional outbursts. Anger becomes the automatic and exaggerated response to any kind of provocation, whether real or perceived.

A child growing up in a household where the parents frequently argue, even if these discussions aren't directed at them, creates a constant state of tension that leads to a heightened state of alertness. The brain, always expecting a new conflict, reacts with anger when any situation of tension arises. Similarly, teenagers who face daily conflicts with friends or teachers may internalize anger as a way to deal with these situations, exploding at any criticism or provocation.

Another scenario can occur in school environments, where a young person is frequently provoked or bullied. Humiliation and constant conflict with peers cause them to develop an aggressive defense response. Anger explodes as a way to protect themselves, often even before the conflict happens, as a way of "*attacking before being attacked.*"

When we carry these experiences into adulthood, we may notice that many of us react with outbursts of anger in everyday situations, especially when we feel that we are being rejected, devalued, or challenged again. Anger arises as an attempt to regain the control and emotional security we feel we lost amid the conflicts. However, this mechanism becomes self-destructive, affecting our relationships, mental health, and our ability to deal with difficulties in a balanced way.

When we look at these outbursts of anger, we can realize that they are, in essence, a reflection of a deep fear of rejection. In the moments when anger explodes, what we are really saying is: "*I don't want to be hurt again, I don't want to feel vulnerable to conflict.*" However, instead of resolving the issue, this behavior ends up creating more distance and escalating the conflicts.

When we grow up in environments where confrontation is the norm, we tend to internalize the idea that the world is a hostile place, and therefore, we need to defend ourselves constantly. Anger becomes a barrier that we build around our deepest emotions, but ironically, it ends up pushing us away from the solutions and connections we seek.

By understanding that our outbursts of anger don't come from nowhere, that they are an automatic response to conflicts that have marked our history, and that now we try to avoid them at all costs, even if often disproportionally, we can begin to reprogram our emotional responses.

We can seek healthier and more constructive ways to handle conflicts, without letting anger take over.

Pause to Reflect

- *How do I react when I receive criticism?*
    - I often defend myself impulsively, responding harshly or distancing myself from the person, even when the intent is constructive.
- *Do I notice disproportionate reactions to criticism?*
    - I explode over trivial situations, such as family arguments or workplace feedback, acting defensively or hostilely.
- *Do past criticisms make me feel insecure?*
    - I avoid sharing ideas or participating in social events out of fear of judgment, even without evidence that it would happen.
- *Do I react disproportionately to minor setbacks?*
    - I lash out in frustration at work or at home, even over small problems like long lines or technical failures.
- *Do my emotional responses push people away?*
    - During arguments, I lose control and end up creating emotional distance, whether with partners, colleagues, or family members.
- *Do I lose emotional control in situations of rejection?*
    - I react impulsively in cases of rejection, such as sending angry messages or isolating myself after receiving negative feedback.

- *Do I feel the need to justify my actions when criticized?*
    - My immediate reaction is to defend myself or list reasons for my behavior, ignoring the value of the feedback.
- *Do I interpret criticism as a personal attack?*
    - Even respectful comments make me feel undervalued, as if my competence or effort is being questioned.
- *Do I avoid situations where I might be evaluated or criticized?*
    - I avoid leading projects or presenting ideas out of fear of seeming inadequate or being subjected to negative judgments.
- *Do criticism or non-praising comments irritate me?*
    - I react defensively or my mood changes when receiving suggestions for improvement, even when constructive.
- *Do comparisons, even implicit ones, trigger irritation?*
    - I feel diminished when others are praised, whether colleagues or family members, even if no direct comparison is made to me.
- *Do minor frustrations irritate me disproportionately?*
    - Trivial situations, such as seeing friends achieve different goals than mine, trigger irritation and negative comments.
- *Do I explode in anger when I feel challenged?*

    - I react with yelling or frustration in situations involving criticism or unexpected decisions, especially at home or work.
- *Do I relive past situations that amplify my anger?*
    - Current conflicts often bring back memories of feeling undervalued or controlled, intensifying my emotional reaction.

When Reactivity Comes to the Surface

The period when my emotional reactivity became most evident—almost jeopardizing my 30-year marriage—happened in the years leading up to my journey of self-discovery, the very journey that now allows me to write this book.

I got married at 21, at a time in my life when I was emotionally shattered. Without realizing it, I brought into my marriage all the defense mechanisms shaped by my hidden wound of rejection over the years. Back then, I had no awareness of this. Only now, after applying the exercises I present in this book, do I understand the gravity of my emotional state at that time.

When we got married, I was unemployed—a situation that lasted for two years. It was only on the eve of our son's birth that, with the help of my wife's aunt, I landed a job as an English teacher at a private school. However, the available hours were scarce, and I had to supplement my income by offering private lessons at home. Even so, the money barely covered our needs.

The lack of financial stability was worsened by my difficulty in dealing with authority figures, such as employers. I remained employed for only a short time before choosing to dedicate myself exclusively to private lessons. We often depended on financial help from my wife's family, which led them, out of concern, to suggest that I look for other job opportunities—even working as a supermarket cashier would pay more than I was earning. To me, these suggestions felt like criticism of my abilities and a devaluation of my potential.

I carried a deep shame about taking on any job that wasn't linked to some form of intellectual skill. I took pride in being an English teacher because learning it at a young age had been, for me, a symbol of distinction. Later, I accepted a job as a hotel receptionist, but only because it required fluency in English. Today, I understand why.

My father, my grandmother's "*perfect son,*" was the only one in the family to leave the countryside, pursue higher education, graduate in Accounting, and later in Law. When my grandmother introduced me, it was always with great emphasis: "*This is Gerson, my grandson, the son of my son, Dr. Edmundo.*" At the time, I didn't grasp the weight of that image. As the first grandchild and son of the "*perfect doctor,*" the implicit expectation was clear: I could be nothing less. This fueled my ego while simultaneously placing a suffocating pressure on me.

With this dynamic, distorted by the defense mechanisms of my hidden wound of rejection, it was only logical that my pride wouldn't allow me to accept any job that didn't confer some kind of intellectual prestige.

Over the years, this mindset led me to reinforce a belief formed in childhood: that I would only be accepted and valued—first by people, and later by my wife and family—if I proved my worth through financial success. After decades of struggle, I finally started making more money. In the last six years, I have been able to provide my wife with a life of comfort and financial freedom that, in her words, she never imagined we would achieve.

In my mind, everything was perfect. The biggest problem we had faced for years—financial insecurity—seemed to be fading away. However, as I climbed this so-called "*ladder of success,*" my wife grew increasingly unhappy. That was when my emotional reactivity surfaced. I simply couldn't understand how she could be unhappy when we were finally living the life of our dreams.

I worked more than 12 hours a day, fully focused on making money. I didn't dedicate quality time to my wife. If she wanted to go to the beach, I gave her money to go with her friends, but I never joined her. We lived in a huge house, yet we spent most of our time alone, in separate spaces. When she tried to tell me how she felt or suggested that we find solutions, I lost control—I yelled, insulted, and unleashed on her all the frustration I had accumulated from decades of financial hardship.

I couldn't see her pain. In my distorted view, I had finally proven my worth to the world. It was time to show off, to spend on family, to buy an expensive car and visit relatives after years, just to prove that the "*broke and indebted guy*" had turned things around.

This desperate need for validation led me to spend everything I earned impulsively. And since money is not something you chase but something you attract, I wasn't emotionally prepared to keep it. Soon, I lost the contracts that had been sustaining us, and the downfall was devastating. At one point, I had to sell our refillable propane cylinder just to buy food.

At that moment, my emotional instability reached its peak. I blamed my children, my relatives, and especially my wife for our situation. I threw harsh and resentful words at her that, in hindsight, only deepened both of our pain. Our marriage was hanging by a thread.

That was the turning point when I decided to embark on my journey of self-discovery. And that decision changed everything. Today, as I write these words, I realize that collapse was the greatest gift life could have given me. It forced me to face my inner demons, to understand the root of my destructive behaviors, and ultimately, to free myself from the burden of my hidden wound of rejection.

To move forward in our journey of self-discovery, it is essential to be deeply honest in observing our daily behavior and identifying the "*routine*" of emotional reactivity. Often, we label this pattern as part of a "*short-tempered personality*" and almost unquestionably believe that we were simply born this way—"*what can you do?*" But is that really true? Were we really born this way?

Only through honest reflection and the courage to confront our ego can we unravel the hidden origins of these behaviors and emotions. This journey of self-discovery requires effort, but it opens the door to profound transformation.

Our next focus will be on distrust and toxic relationships—another set of behaviors that deeply impact our emotional well-being and our connections with others.

9

DISTRUST AND TOXIC RELATIONSHIPS

Distrust and toxic relationships develop as defense mechanisms when the wound of rejection stems from broken promises, emotional betrayals, psychological violence, disrespect, or abandonment.

These behaviors arise to prevent us from reliving past suffering, but ironically, they lead us to repeat it unconsciously. Excessive distrust, for example, can stem from frustration with broken promises, creating constant vigilance in relationships, where we see threats even in the most innocent intentions. The fear of being deceived or betrayed becomes so intense that it undermines the foundation of any healthy bond.

Pathological jealousy also falls into this category. When we experience emotional betrayals, our self-confidence and sense of security shatter, leading us to project this fear of loss and deception onto every intimate interaction. This creates an atmosphere of control and insecurity, corroding the trust that is essential for lasting relationships.

Another common pattern is the tendency to enter abusive relationships. Those exposed to psychological violence or disrespect may unconsciously accept or even seek relationships that reflect this dynamic. Familiarity with abuse can create the illusion that this type of relationship is normal or deserved, perpetuating the cycle of pain.

Finally, relational paranoia arises as a result of experiences of abandonment. When we are abandoned emotionally or physically, we develop an extreme sensitivity to any sign of distance or rejection. This constant fear of losing the other person leads us to interpret even the smallest gestures as indicators of betrayal or lack of commitment.

These defense mechanisms keep us trapped in cycles of suffering. We need to recognize how these emotional responses were formed, and by understanding their origins, we can reprogram our reactions and cultivate relationships based on trust, respect, and self-love, freeing ourselves from the toxic cycles that imprison us.

Excessive Distrust

Excessive distrust is a defense mechanism that arises in response to the hidden wound of rejection caused by broken promises. We have all experienced moments when our expectations were frustrated, and when this happens repeatedly—especially in childhood—our ability to trust is deeply shaken. To protect ourselves from the pain of further disappointments, we develop a tendency to distrust those around us, creating emotional barriers that prevent us from forming genuine connections.

This behavior is often triggered by experiences of broken promises during vulnerable stages of life. In childhood, we rely heavily on the words and assurances of the adults around us. A typical example is when a parent promises to spend more time with their child but ends up prioritizing other tasks. While this may seem insignificant, to the child, the unfulfilled promise can create feelings of abandonment and insecurity. Over time, the brain begins to associate promises with disappointment, planting the seed of distrust.

Another common example is the promise of emotional stability in a relationship—such as a couple assuring each other they will always stay together, only to break up for various reasons. This type of rupture can deepen preexisting emotional wounds, making the person feel the need to remain constantly on guard in future relationships, always anticipating the next betrayal or broken commitment.

In professional life, a boss who promises a promotion or an opportunity for growth but never delivers reinforces the belief that the world is unpredictable and that people's words cannot be trusted.

This pattern of excessive distrust is an attempt to protect ourselves from the pain we have already experienced. However, by staying in a constant state of alertness, we end up sabotaging our own relationships, building a wall that prevents us from embracing new experiences and fully trusting others. Although this behavior originates from a legitimate need for emotional protection, persistent distrust isolates us and keeps us from enjoying healthier, more fulfilling relationships.

Pathological Jealousy

When we talk about pathological jealousy, we are referring to a behavior that goes beyond the natural insecurity that many of us may feel in certain situations. Jealousy, in its pathological state, emerges as yet another defense mechanism against the constant fear of being betrayed—not just physically, but more profoundly, emotionally. This type of jealousy is born from a hidden wound of rejection, where promises of affection, loyalty, or presence were not fulfilled.

At its core, pathological jealousy is a response to what we call "*emotional betrayals*." These are moments when, in childhood or adolescence, we felt that someone we trusted broke that bond, making us perceive that we are not important enough. Over time, this feeling solidifies into a constant fear that the people we love or engage with will eventually abandon us or prefer someone else. As a result, we begin to closely monitor the actions of those around us, always searching for signs of disloyalty—even when none exist.

A child who felt emotionally abandoned by a parent—one who promised to be present for an important event, such as a school performance, but failed to show up—experiences this absence as a sign that their parent's love or attention is insufficient. Over time, this child may come to believe that other people's love is unstable and unreliable. In adulthood, this fear of being emotionally neglected can manifest as excessive jealousy in romantic relationships.

A teenager who has always been loyal to their friends but later discovers they were excluded from an important gathering or spoken about behind their back may perceive this as an emotional betrayal. The feeling of being replaced or undervalued creates insecurity in future relationships. As an adult, this person may constantly feel that they will be left out by friends or romantic partners, leading to jealousy and distrust—even when there is no apparent reason.

We can also observe emotional betrayals within family dynamics. When siblings are constantly compared, and one of them always feels overlooked, the child who grows up feeling "*less loved*" or "*less special*" may carry the belief that, in any future relationship, they will always be the less important choice. This can lead to possessive and jealous behaviors as they try to ensure they won't be left behind again.

In adult romantic relationships, an emotional betrayal can occur when a partner begins to dedicate more time and attention to another person or activity—such as work, friends, or even social media. Even without physical infidelity, this shift in attention can be interpreted as a direct threat to the emotional bond. For someone who already carries a hidden wound of rejection, this becomes a powerful trigger for pathological jealousy, leading them to demand increasing proof of love and loyalty in an attempt to soothe their internal insecurity.

Pathological jealousy is, therefore, a "*protective routine*" we create to avoid reliving the devastating feelings of rejection, replacement, or emotional loss. However, instead of offering protection, this behavior ends up sabotaging the very relationships we wish to preserve. By constantly demanding proof of love and obsessively monitoring our partner's actions, we undermine trust and the health of the relationship—ultimately creating the emotional distance and rejection we fear the most.

Exploring pathological jealousy is, at its core, an invitation to look inward and confront our experiences of emotional betrayal. We must recognize that while our fears are valid, they are rooted in old wounds that cannot be healed by controlling others' behavior.

Tendency Toward Abusive Relationships

Throughout our lives, we may have experienced the pain of rejection, often manifesting in subtle yet harmful ways, such as psychological violence. This violence can take shape through words and actions that make us feel small, as if we are not enough, creating a behavioral pattern that leads us to develop a tendency to enter abusive relationships. This dynamic may seem like a way to cope with emotional pain, but in reality, it becomes a defense mechanism that perpetuates suffering.

Psychological violence is insidious and can appear in many forms. A negative word, a disapproving look, or the silent treatment can wound more deeply than a physical blow. In childhood, we may have experienced moments where our self-esteem was hurt—perhaps when a parent or guardian compared us unfavorably to a sibling or peer, leaving us with a sense of inadequacy. These experiences push us to seek validation in relationships, even when they are harmful. We may come to believe that love must be earned at the expense of our own dignity.

Psychological Violence

- In our childhood, constant comparisons to our siblings or peers made us feel that the only way to be accepted was to meet an unattainable standard.
- In romantic relationships, we may have heard phrases from our partners like, "*You never do anything right*" or "*No one else will want you.*" These constant criticisms not only undermine our self-esteem but also make us dependent on the love of someone who belittles us.
- We recall moments when we were subjected to the silent treatment from a parent—who, instead of communicating, withdrew emotionally whenever we made a mistake. This taught us that love is conditional and that we must strive to avoid disapproval, which can lead us to tolerate abuse in search of validation.
- We may also have faced situations where we were made to feel responsible for someone else's happiness. "*If you really loved me, you would do what I say.*" These manipulations lead us to believe that the blame is ours, perpetuating a cycle of abuse.

These examples illustrate how psychological violence, often invisible, can shape our behaviors and lead us into abusive relationships. Over time, we may become so accustomed to pain that we begin to see it as a normal part of love. Only by recognizing these patterns and uncovering their origins can we reprogram them, break free from harmful behaviors, and learn to value ourselves—establishing relationships that are healthy and respectful.

Relational Paranoia

Relational paranoia emerges as a defense mechanism when the hidden wound of rejection stems from experiences of abandonment. As human beings, we are wired to seek emotional connections, and the mere thought of losing these connections can be distressing. When we go through situations that make us feel we might be abandoned, we develop excessive vigilance over our relationships. This constant distrust can lead us to interpret the actions and behaviors of others as threats to our emotional security.

Experiences of Abandonment

In childhood, when our parents argued or separated, we were left with a sense of insecurity, making us believe we were not important enough to keep the family together. This initial experience can create a pattern in which we associate any small sign of disinterest or distance as a precursor to inevitable abandonment.

In adolescence, when close friends began making new friendships or drifting away, we reinforced the belief that we were less valuable or unable to maintain connections. This fuels the paranoia that any new friend can easily replace us.

In adulthood, we may feel insecure when a partner receives a message from a friend, interpreting the interaction as a sign of disinterest. This distorted perception can lead us to act possessively, resulting in unnecessary conflicts and straining the relationship.

In the workplace, we may experience a sense of abandonment from colleagues or superiors. A negative piece of feedback may be interpreted as a sign that we no longer belong to the team, reinforcing our defensive and distrustful behavior. This cycle feeds itself, as our paranoia can create a hostile environment, pushing away the very people we want to keep close.

In past relationships, betrayal or broken trust may have left deep wounds, planting the seed of relational paranoia. This leads us to distrust not only romantic partners but all significant relationships in our lives. As a result, we begin to interpret neutral actions as potential threats, reinforcing our belief that abandonment is inevitable.

In summary, relational paranoia is a reflection of our deepest fears of abandonment. It is a defense mechanism that traps us in a cycle of distrust and loneliness.

Attraction to Destructive Relationships

When we look back at our childhood and adolescence, we often find the roots of the attraction to destructive relationships that we experience in adulthood. The way we learn to love and be loved is deeply influenced by the experiences and family dynamics we go through in our early years.

Children who grow up in homes where love is accompanied by criticism, rejection, or even emotional absence tend to develop a hidden wound of rejection. As a defense mechanism, their minds create distorted beliefs about what it means to be loved. For example, a child who desperately seeks the attention of an emotionally unavailable parent may internalize the idea that love must be earned and that they will never be enough. In adulthood, this same child may feel drawn to partners who recreate this dynamic of emotional distance and invalidate their feelings, perpetuating a cycle of emotional pain.

Similarly, young people who grow up hearing harsh words or witnessing constant arguments between their parents may associate love with conflict or disrespect. For example, a teenager who repeatedly sees their father belittling their mother may, without realizing it, start to believe that disrespect and love go hand in hand. When seeking relationships in adulthood, this pattern may repeat itself, making disrespect feel familiar and, in a way, comfortable.

In other cases, emotional neglect can have an equally profound impact. A child whose emotions were constantly ignored or invalidated by their caregivers may grow up believing that their emotional needs do not matter. As a result, they may attract partners who reinforce this belief, creating relationships where their emotions are dismissed, and they constantly have to fight for recognition.

These patterns are not conscious choices. They stem from an unconscious attempt to recreate and perhaps correct the painful scenarios of childhood. However, by repeating these dynamics, we only reinforce the same emotional wounds, keeping ourselves trapped in destructive relationships.

Recognizing the origin of this attraction is the first step in breaking the cycle. When we identify these patterns, we can begin to question them and replace them with new beliefs—beliefs that allow us to seek relationships where we are truly seen, respected, and loved. After all, we deserve a love that nourishes us, not one that consumes us.

Pause to Reflect

Reflecting on this set of behaviors and emotions requires courage to revisit old wounds—wounds long buried in the depths of the subconscious and guarded under lock and key. However, if you have made it this far, trust yourself: the strength and "*muscles*" you have developed in the previous chapters are ready to support you through this process. Move forward, without fear!

- *Do I distrust the intentions of those around me, even when there are no clear signs that they will disappoint me?*
    - At work, do I question whether my colleagues genuinely support my ideas or if they are trying to sabotage me?
    - In romantic relationships, do I feel like my partner might be hiding something, even without concrete reasons?
    - Do I avoid sharing personal information with friends for fear that they might use it against me?
- *Do I prefer to do everything on my own because I believe others will always fail or not follow through on their promises?*
    - At work, do I avoid delegating tasks, even when I am overwhelmed?
- *Do I react with frustration when someone fails to keep a promise, even if the situation is beyond their control?*
    - Do I get irritated when a friend or partner cancels plans, interpreting it as a lack of consideration or interest?
- *How do I react when my partner spends time with other people?*
    - Do I feel anxious and imagine there might be something more than just friendship?
    - Do I feel the need to know the details of their interactions with colleagues or friends?
- *Do I often compare my relationship to those of others?*

  - When I see couples on social media, do I start questioning whether my relationship is as good as theirs?
  - Do I compare my partner's displays of affection with those of other couples?
- *How do I deal with my insecurities about my appearance or self-worth?*
  - Do I feel uncomfortable when my partner compliments someone else, questioning my attractiveness?
  - Do I interpret my partner's distractions as a lack of interest in me?
- *How do I react when I feel undervalued in a relationship?*
  - Do I ignore my needs to avoid conflict, even if it makes me unhappy?
  - Do I try to please my partner at all costs, compromising my values?

- *What signs of abuse do I ignore?*
  - Do I accept sarcastic or dismissive comments as "*jokes*"?
  - Do I avoid confronting my partner about behaviors that make me anxious or insecure?
- *Have I ever felt trapped in cycles of abusive relationships?*
  - Do I notice that I attract partners with toxic behaviors similar to those in past relationships?
  - Do I justify abusive behaviors, believing that they will improve over time?

- *How do my experiences of abandonment influence my perception of current relationships?*
    - Do I feel easily excluded or replaced, even without clear evidence?
- *Do I interpret other people's actions as threats to my emotional security?*
    - Do I see criticism or someone else's need for space as rejection or a lack of love?
    - When someone doesn't respond immediately, do I feel anxious and distrustful?
- *How do I react when I sense that someone close to me might be pulling away?*
    - Do I try to overly please them to prevent them from leaving?
    - Do I become defensive or avoid discussing problems out of fear of losing them?
- *How have moments of disrespect shaped my expectations in relationships?*
    - Have experiences of exclusion or devaluation led me to believe that I must accept relationships where I am not respected?
- *Does my need for validation lead me to accept disrespectful behavior?*
    - Do I accept destructive criticism or possessive behaviors as signs of care or love?
    - Do I tolerate offensive jokes or constant interruptions, believing that I must put up with them?
- *What behavioral patterns do I maintain that perpetuate destructive relationships?*

- Do I choose partners with traits similar to those who have disrespected me in the past?
- Do I avoid confrontation, sacrificing my emotional well-being to maintain peace?
- Do I ignore red flags, believing that I deserve this kind of treatment?

Diving deeper into these behavioral patterns is a sign of great courage and commitment to your journey of self-discovery. You should be proud—few people have the strength and determination to face their ego and recognize the areas that need transformation in order to rebuild their emotional and behavioral framework.

Next, we will explore the seventh and final stage of this journey: the "*routine*" of self-expression and creativity.

10

SELF-EXPRESSION AND CREATIVITY

Self-expression and creativity are fundamental components of the human experience, serving as essential channels for communicating feelings, ideas, and unique perspectives. When we express ourselves authentically, we not only connect with others but also develop a sense of identity and purpose. However, achieving this freedom of expression is not always easy.

Various factors can inhibit our ability to express ourselves creatively. The fear of rejection and disapproval—whether from family figures or society at large—often prevents us from exploring our artistic potential. Criticism of our creative expressions can lead to creative blocks, resulting in frustration and the feeling that our ideas lack value. Additionally, the absence of encouragement or stimulation can contribute to the suppression of talents, leading us to conform to what is accepted or expected rather than pursuing our passions.

Artistic insecurity becomes an additional obstacle, making us doubt our abilities and the quality of our work. This cycle of insecurity and fear not only limits personal expression but also stifles the creative potential that resides within each of us. In the following sections, we will explore each of these behaviors in detail.

Creative Block

Creative block is a phenomenon familiar to many of us. In a world that values originality and self-expression, the experience of feeling unable to create can be deeply frustrating. However, this blockage often stems from a defense mechanism developed when the wound of rejection arises from criticism of our creative expression. Throughout our journey, we learn to associate the act of creating something new and authentic with the risk of rejection.

When we reflect on the experiences that shaped our relationship with creativity, we can identify moments when criticism from others impacted our willingness to express ourselves. For example, we may have shared a painting, a poem, or a song with friends or family, only to receive comments that, instead of encouraging us, undermined our confidence. A phrase like "*This looks terrible*" or "*You need to improve a lot*" can become a deep wound, leading us to question our artistic worth and suppress our creativity.

Another common situation occurs in academic or professional environments, where the pressure for a perfect outcome is constant. If a teacher or colleague criticizes our work without offering constructive feedback, it can make us feel like our ideas are insignificant, leading to creative block. The sense that our expressions are not valued can cause us to hesitate to try again, creating a cycle of inhibition.

Furthermore, in some cultures and families, emotional and creative expression may be discouraged. If we grew up in an environment where creativity was seen as a sign of weakness or frivolity, we learned to suppress our creative impulses. We may have heard phrases like "*What you're doing won't get you anywhere*" or "*You should focus on something more practical.*" Such comments can internalize the belief that being creative is risky, leading to the development of a block that prevents us from accessing our full potential.

From the moment we realize that our artistic expressions can be judged or devalued, we create a "*routine*" to avoid the pain of rejection. By identifying this routine, we can reprogram it, unlock our creative potential, and rediscover the joy of creating without fear of criticism.

Fear of Self-Expression

When we talk about the fear of self-expression, we encounter a deeply rooted theme in our experiences and family interactions. This fear often emerges as a defense mechanism, shaped by the hidden wound of rejection that arises when we face family disapproval. Throughout life, we learn that expressing our feelings, opinions, and talents can expose us to judgment and criticism, leading many of us to choose silence or to hide our true identities.

In childhood, many of us experienced moments when our expressions were discouraged or criticized. This could have manifested in various ways—such as a dismissive remark about a school performance, criticism of our artistic abilities, or even a lack of support when sharing our dreams and aspirations. These experiences accumulate over time, creating a paralyzing fear that prevents us from expressing ourselves freely.

For example, when trying to share a new idea at a family gathering, we may have been interrupted or ridiculed, reinforcing the belief that our opinions hold no value. Such rejection can be deeply painful, making us feel invisible or unrecognized. The same happens when we present a project or achievement and, instead of receiving encouragement, we are met with discouraging criticism.

Additionally, we may have faced situations where expressing our emotions was met with indifference or, worse, disapproval. Imagine a teenager opening up about their insecurities, only to become the target of jokes or contempt from family members. These moments leave lasting marks and shape our relationship with self-expression, leading us to suppress our emotions to avoid the pain of rejection.

This need for protection pushes us toward conformity, where we feel compelled to mold ourselves to others' expectations. As a result, we set aside our talents, passions, and opinions in an attempt to avoid criticism. Over time, we become increasingly disconnected from who we truly are, creating a block in our ability to express ourselves authentically.

This fear also translates into missed opportunities. For instance, an artist who hesitates to showcase their work out of fear of judgment may lose the chance to be recognized and appreciated. A student who refuses to participate in classroom discussions for fear of sounding foolish may limit their learning and growth. This dynamic harms not only our self-image but also our ability to connect and interact meaningfully with others.

Therefore, as we reflect on the fear of self-expression, it is essential to recognize that it is often fueled by past experiences of disapproval. We must understand that true freedom of expression is a right we should all pursue, regardless of the circumstances. By allowing ourselves to be vulnerable and authentic, we can break free from the chains that hold us back and open ourselves to a world of possibilities—where our voices can finally be heard and valued.

Talent Inhibition

Talent inhibition is a subtle yet powerful psychological defense mechanism that develops when we feel that our abilities or gifts were not properly encouraged or recognized. This mechanism takes shape when we perceive rejection in the form of a lack of support during key moments in our lives, especially in childhood and adolescence. Without the necessary encouragement, we begin to believe that our abilities are neither important nor worthy of exploration, leading us to suppress our own talents.

As creative and expressive beings, each of us possesses unique abilities—whether in artistic, scientific, athletic, or intellectual fields. However, when these abilities are not valued or nurtured by those around us—such as family, friends, teachers, or mentors—we start to doubt our own competence. As a result, we often choose safer, more conventional paths, leaving behind the true potential that resides within us.

The lack of encouragement can manifest in many ways: when our efforts are ignored, when our creativity is not appreciated, or even when we are not given opportunities to explore our skills. Over time, this absence of support creates an internal barrier, where we become our own censors, limiting ourselves to repetitive behaviors that do not challenge our capabilities.

Lack of Encouragement Leading to Talent Inhibition

Imagine a young person with a natural talent for music. From an early age, they show an aptitude for playing instruments, but instead of receiving support to develop this passion, their parents dismiss it as a meaningless hobby, urging them to focus on more "*secure*" or "*profitable*" careers. Over time, this young musician begins to abandon their craft, suppressing their talent simply because they lack the encouragement to believe that this ability could lead to something meaningful.

Another example can be seen in someone with a talent for solving complex problems creatively—perhaps in fields like mathematics or science. If this person is not encouraged to explore their intellectual curiosity—whether due to uninspiring teachers or a lack of programs that stimulate this type of intelligence—they may give up on pursuing an innovative career, conforming to paths that demand less creativity and skill.

Talent inhibition also occurs in more subtle areas, such as leadership skills. A person with the potential to influence and lead may be discouraged by an environment where their ideas are constantly ignored or dismissed. The lack of opportunities to develop this ability can lead them to doubt their own capabilities, causing them to avoid situations where their talents could shine.

When we realize that our abilities are not valued, we often choose not to take risks to avoid further disappointment or discouragement. Instead of facing this feeling of rejection head-on, we retreat, convincing ourselves that we are not good enough or that our talents are not worth exploring.

This defense mechanism, over time, deprives us of a richer and more meaningful life—one where we could use our gifts not only to transform our own experiences but also to positively impact those around us.

Reversing talent inhibition requires a reevaluation of how we interpret past encouragement—or the lack of it—and the courage to confront the fear of rejection that holds us back. After all, the world may not have given us the support we needed, but we still have the power to recognize and value our own talents, even if only for ourselves.

The first step is to acknowledge that this inhibition is a defense mechanism. While it may have served a purpose at some point in our lives, it no longer needs to control us. By confronting and reprogramming this "*routine*," we can finally allow our talents to flourish—without waiting for the external validation that never came.

Conformism

Conformism is a behavior that emerges as a defense mechanism when the wound of rejection arises from failing to meet expectations—whether those of our parents, teachers, peers, or even our own. It stems from the shame of failure and, in many cases, the constant sense that our efforts are never enough. When we see ourselves as incapable of achieving what is expected of us, our natural reaction may be to stop trying altogether, settling for what feels safe or comfortable, even if that path brings neither satisfaction nor personal fulfillment.

We grow up hearing what we must do to "*be successful*," "*be accepted*," or "*make our parents proud*." However, when these standards become unattainable, the pressure can push us toward conformism as a form of refuge. By accepting less than what we truly desire or are capable of achieving, we convince ourselves that it is better not to try at all than to risk more frustration or disappointment. In doing so, we suppress our true potential.

There are countless examples of how failing to meet expectations can lead to conformism. Imagine someone who has always been told they should pursue a career in law because it is stable and respected, even though their true passion lies in psychology. Constant comparisons with siblings who followed traditional career paths may lead this person to resign themselves to a mediocre professional life, lacking the courage to pursue their true calling.

Another example involves a child who excels in sports, but whose parents place greater importance on academic achievements. Over time, the child may abandon sports altogether, conforming to the idea that their passion is not valued and following a path that does not bring them fulfillment.

In the workplace, conformism can manifest when an innovative employee repeatedly sees their ideas dismissed or criticized. Feeling incapable of meeting leadership's expectations, they eventually decide to simply follow the rules, doing the bare minimum to keep their job but lacking engagement or motivation.

In personal relationships, conformism can arise in someone who, after experiencing heartbreak or disappointment, convinces themselves that they are unworthy of a healthy relationship. As a result, they settle for less than they deserve, remaining in an unfulfilling relationship that feels "*safe*" and "*convenient*."

When we fail to meet the expectations placed upon us—whether by others or ourselves—conformism becomes a way to shield ourselves from the pain of rejection. However, in doing so, we also sacrifice our passions, our authenticity, and the chance to live a more fulfilling life. Thus, conformism is not only a defense against frustration but also a barrier that prevents us from exploring our true potential and creating a path that aligns with who we really are.

Artistic Insecurity

Artistic insecurity is a common phenomenon, especially among those who, at some point in life, have experienced harsh criticism of their creative abilities or talents. More often than not, the root of this insecurity lies in a deep-seated defense mechanism triggered by hidden wound of rejection. When our artistic expression—whether painting, music, writing, or any other creative talent—is criticized, we internalize it as a direct threat to our self-esteem. This feeling of rejection becomes an emotional trap that blocks us from fully expressing our creativity.

When we are criticized for something as personal as our art or skills, we interpret it as a rejection of our identity. After all, what we create is an extension of who we are. If a part of us is criticized or undervalued, it is natural to want to protect ourselves from that pain. This is where artistic insecurity arises—a way of shielding ourselves from future criticism or disapproval.

We convince ourselves that it might be better not to put ourselves out there, that we are "*not talented enough*" to try again, or that other people's opinions matter more than our own desire to create. This insecurity is fueled by the need to avoid the pain of rejection and the fear of experiencing the judgment that has often been unfairly imposed on us.

Criticism That Fuels Artistic Insecurity

There are many scenarios in which criticism can plant the seed of insecurity. Let's explore a few examples:

- In childhood, when we drew or painted, but our parents or teachers told us it wasn't good. These criticisms, though often unintentional, can have a lasting impact. Comments like "*You were never good at drawing*" or "*That doesn't look like what it's supposed to be*" may seem harmless, but they echo in our minds as a warning that we should never try again.
- Among friends or at school, where we felt judged when attempting creative activities. Perhaps during a theater performance or singing in public for the first time, we were ridiculed by our peers. This kind of social criticism can leave a deep scar, making us avoid any future situation where we might be judged again.
- Within the family, when we tried to learn something new, like playing an instrument or practicing a sport, only to be discouraged by negative comments. If we grow up hearing things like "*This isn't for you*" or "*Don't bother trying, you don't have talent*", we internalize these messages as absolute truths. This makes us hesitant to pursue any skill that involves the risk of failure or public exposure.
- In professional environments, when our creative ideas are constantly rejected or undervalued. Perhaps at work, you suggested an innovative approach or presented a creative solution to a problem, only to be dismissed or ignored. These experiences reinforce the

belief that our skills and talents are not valuable, leading to a downward spiral of insecurity.

The result of these experiences of rejection is a "*routine*" of creative withdrawal. We begin to retreat into our comfort zone, avoiding exposure, limiting our creative expression, and stalling the development of our skills. This can manifest in many ways: procrastination, fear of starting new projects, self-sabotage, or even the complete abandonment of any creative pursuit.

What makes this cycle dangerous is that it feeds itself. The more we avoid putting ourselves out there, the more we convince ourselves that we are incapable or unworthy. This erodes our confidence and traps us in a constant state of self-doubt.

Artistic insecurity does not have to be a life sentence. We can use it as an opportunity to rediscover ourselves, rebuild our confidence, and gradually expand our capacity for expression. After all, true art is not about perfection but about the courage to express oneself. And that courage can be cultivated when we decide that we will no longer be prisoners of the fear of rejection or criticism.

Pause to Reflect

- *What past experiences do I associate with my fear of creating?*
    - A childhood teacher devalued my art project, and that still echoes in my memories.

- Family and friends have made jokes about something I created, leading me to keep my ideas to myself.

- *Do I frequently compare myself to others in terms of creative ability?*
  - Seeing talented artists on social media makes me feel like my work will never be good enough.
  - I often avoid participating in exhibitions because I believe my creations won't be as valued as others'.
- *Do I avoid sharing my opinions or feelings for fear of being criticized or rejected?*
  - In work meetings, I often remain silent even when I know my idea could improve the project.
  - In discussions about topics important to me, I prefer not to speak up to avoid conflict or judgment.
- *Do I suppress my creativity or artistic talents for fear of criticism?*
  - I have written songs and poems but never shared them for fear of being undervalued.
  - On social media, I avoid posting creative videos or photos, worried that others might judge me negatively.
- *Do I feel the need to change or adapt my opinions to please others?*
  - In family gatherings, I end up agreeing with the majority to avoid being '*the different one*'.

    - I follow workplace expectations rather than presenting my creative ideas, even when I feel they would be better.
- *Do I feel that my skills have not been valued, leading me to abandon them?*
    - I gave up playing the guitar because my family said music had no future.
- *Do I avoid situations where my skills could be exposed for fear of criticism?*
    - Even though I enjoy public speaking, I avoid events for fear of criticism.
    - I wanted to participate in artistic contests but backed out, thinking my work wouldn't be good enough.
- *Do I feel frustrated for not exploring my talents, but believe it's too late?*
    - I'd love to return to photography, but I feel I've lost my touch and the right moment for it.
    - I once dreamed of working in a creative field, but now I believe I lack the time or resources to invest in it.
- *Do I give up on my desires and dreams because they don't align with others' expectations?*
    - I wanted to study literature but chose engineering to meet my family's expectations.
    - I remain in a relationship without connection because I fear judgment for being single.
- *Do I avoid trying new things for fear of not meeting others' expectations?*
    - I always wanted to learn to dance but gave up because friends thought it was strange.

    - I have innovative ideas at work but never present them for fear of seeming too unconventional.
- *Do I accept less than I desire for fear of disappointing others?*
    - I stay in a frustrating job because my parents value stability more than my happiness.
    - I dream of traveling the world but gave up because I don't want my family to feel abandoned.
- *Do I avoid sharing my creations for fear of being judged?*
    - I've never published my writings, fearing no one would find them interesting.
- *Do I often compare myself to others and feel I'm never good enough?*
    - When colleagues receive praise for their creative ideas, I feel like I'll never reach the same level.
- *Do I give up on creative projects for fear of not achieving perfection?*
    - I've abandoned unfinished paintings because I thought they would never be good enough.
    - I avoid starting new projects at work because I fear they won't be well-received unless they're perfect.

We have now completed our discussion on the sets of behaviors and feelings that hidden wound of rejection creates as defense mechanisms, attempting to shield us from the pain felt at the moment these "*routines*" were formed.

When I went through this process of self-discovery and realized that these behaviors—which I had believed to be part of my personality and, consequently, my identity—were actually strategies my brain had developed to protect me from the pain of feeling rejected, I was overwhelmed with emotions.

The first feeling I experienced was revolt. I felt betrayed and deceived by myself when I understood that, just like the character George McFly, my life could have taken a completely different path. I thought about how many possibilities and potential I could have explored. However, I was soon overcome by deep relief and a sense of lightness when I realized that these mechanisms were not truly "*me*." They were merely automatic programs, and now that I was aware of them, I had the power to reprogram these "*routines,*" upgrade my system, and begin writing a new story for my life.

I hope you are feeling something similar. This realization is liberating and marks a turning point in your journey.

Before we explore the tools to reprogram these defense "*routines*" that have had such a profound impact on our lives, it is essential to take one more step. Let's dive into a new set of behaviors that arise as a side effect of the cycle created by these defense mechanisms: escapism and addictions.

11

ESCAPISM AND ADDICTIONS

When the Wound of Rejection Pushes Us Toward Unconscious Escapes

When we operate on autopilot, acting based on behavioral patterns deeply ingrained by the wound of rejection, we unknowingly follow defensive mechanisms that lead us into repetitive cycles of undesirable outcomes. It is common to wonder why we continue to experience the same frustrations despite believing we are making the right choices. However, the decisions we perceive as rational are, in reality, shaped by unconscious defense mechanisms designed to shield us from the pain of rejection.

Since we are unaware of the origins of our behaviors and emotions, we often seek relief in ways that initially seem comforting but ultimately reinforce a sense of dissatisfaction and emptiness. These escapist behaviors are attempts to flee from unhealed emotional wounds, masking pain through activities or substances that offer only an illusion of relief. Yet, this relentless pursuit of temporary comfort often leads to dependencies and addictions that imprison us.

In this chapter, we will transition from understanding the defensive behaviors discussed earlier to a deeper analysis of the seven primary escapist behaviors we adopt in response to the hidden wound of rejection. We will explore how these behaviors develop, why they seem so irresistible, and how they fail to resolve the underlying issue, merely numbing it for a while. The behaviors we will examine include substance abuse, compulsive eating, work addiction, smoking, excessive social media use, self-harm, and compulsive shopping.

Each of these behaviors is not merely a "*bad habit*" or a "*lack of willpower*." They are, in fact, coping mechanisms designed to dull pain and avoid confronting deep-seated wounds of rejection. They are the ways we have learned to deal with discomfort, often becoming so ingrained that it is difficult to imagine life without them. We will uncover how these addictions and compulsions serve as "*escape valves*" that, in reality, only reinforce the pain we seek to avoid.

Exploring these seven behaviors is an invitation to break free from the cycle of escapism and begin addressing what truly troubles us. By analyzing them, you will be able to identify where these patterns exist in your life and how they have become disguised methods of escaping the emotional pain of rejection.

By confronting escapism honestly and directly, we gain the opportunity to move beyond temporary relief and embark on a path of true transformation. This chapter bridges the understanding we have developed about defensive behaviors with a more focused approach to forms of escape. It is a call for you to abandon the illusion of comfort found in escapism and courageously face the root of the problem. Now is the time to transform pain into a path toward growth and freedom.

Substance Abuse
(Alcohol and Drugs)

Substance abuse, including alcohol and drugs, often begins subtly and may initially seem like a harmless way to relieve stress or "*unwind*" after a difficult day. However, for someone struggling with the hidden wound of rejection, these substances are more than just occasional escapes or sources of entertainment—they become a means to numb emotional pain and alleviate the deep discomfort that feels unbearable. The urge to escape overwhelming feelings of inadequacy, insecurity, or even a constant sense of emptiness drives individuals to seek substances that offer temporary comfort and relief.

This escapist behavior arises as an immediate coping mechanism for emotional distress. Instead of confronting difficult emotions and working through them at their root, alcohol and drugs provide a quick escape, diverting attention from discomfort and creating a temporary illusion of well-being. However, over time, substance use can intensify, evolving into a dangerous and repetitive pattern of behavior. What initially seemed like a temporary solution turns into a constant need, leading the individual to rely more and more on substances just to cope with life.

While substance use may seem to offer short-term relief, it comes at a steep cost. Alcohol and drug abuse do not resolve underlying problems—instead, they exacerbate them. The feelings of rejection and inadequacy remain buried beneath the effects of intoxication, waiting to resurface once the substances wear off. This leads to a destructive cycle where individuals need to consume more and more to achieve the same effect, increasing the risks of both physical and psychological dependence.

Furthermore, continued substance use can have severe consequences in all areas of life. Relationships with family and friends deteriorate, work or academic performance declines, and physical and mental health suffer. The person seeking to escape emotional pain ends up accumulating even more suffering, fueling a vicious cycle that becomes increasingly difficult to break.

The true path to healing lies in identifying and understanding the emotional triggers that drive substance use and adopting healthier ways to cope with these feelings. Transformation begins by abandoning escapist methods and embracing strategies that foster genuine emotional healing.

Pause to Reflect

The reflection exercises in this section will undoubtedly be a challenge of their own. Even with all the self-awareness you've developed in previous chapters, this stage of your journey will be a true battle between the person you are becoming and the ego, which has been strengthened by years of powerful defense mechanisms. But do not fear! You are ready. Trust yourself and move forward, without hesitation!

And remember: always take notes. Writing down your thoughts helps your mind stay focused on the goal and brings clarity to what is emerging in your transformation process.

1) *Do I resort to alcohol or drugs as a way to cope with difficult or stressful situations in my life?*

- After a heated argument with a loved one, do I feel the need to drink to calm down and forget the problem?
- When I feel overwhelmed at work or school, do I turn to substances to "*relax*" or disconnect for a moment?
- In social events, do I feel that I can only loosen up or have fun if I am under the influence of alcohol or drugs?
- Whenever a feeling of sadness or emptiness arises, do I seek substances to push away the emotional discomfort, even knowing that the relief is temporary?

2) *Do I recognize that substance use has negatively impacted different areas of my life?*

- Has my productivity at work or school significantly declined, and do I justify it by thinking that I need substances to deal with the pressure?
- Have my personal relationships become more tense or distant, and have I noticed that alcohol or drug use contributes to conflicts?

- Do I avoid certain commitments or responsibilities because I know I won't be in a condition to fulfill them due to substance use the night before?
- Has my physical health deteriorated (*sleep problems, weight gain, or other symptoms*), but I continue using substances to try to control the discomfort?

3) *Do I use substances to avoid facing uncomfortable feelings or emotionally challenging situations?*

- When I realize that an important problem needs to be addressed, do I feel the urge to distract myself by drinking or using drugs to "*not think about it now*"?
- When dealing with feelings of rejection or failure, do I seek to numb myself instead of trying to understand and process these emotions?
- Do I struggle to confront family or personal issues and prefer to use substances to forget about difficulties for a while?
- Do situations that bring up old insecurities or unresolved traumas make me feel like I can only handle them under the influence of substances?

Compulsive Eating

For those who carry the hidden wound of rejection, compulsive eating can be an unconscious way of trying to deal with emotional pain. When internal discomfort feels unbearable, overeating provides a momentary relief. Foods—especially those rich in sugar, fat, and carbohydrates—activate the brain's pleasure centers, creating a temporary sense of comfort and fulfillment.

Compulsive eating emerges as a way to numb negative feelings such as sadness, anxiety, loneliness, or frustration. For those who feel rejected, eating may seem like an escape valve to fill an emotional void, compensate for a lack of love or acceptance, or simply distract from uncomfortable thoughts and emotions. Over time, the habit of turning to food as a means of escape transforms into a repetitive and harmful cycle, where the person uses eating to cope with difficult situations or unpleasant feelings, but soon after, feels even worse for having lost control.

This escapist behavior brings serious consequences. Weight gain, low self-esteem, and health problems related to obesity are just some of the possible outcomes. Additionally, the guilt and shame felt after episodes of compulsive eating only intensify the cycle of self-aversion and rejection, creating a scenario where the person feels the need to seek comfort in food again.

It can also have a significant impact on social and professional life. An individual may start avoiding social situations due to embarrassment about their appearance, leading to even greater isolation. The lack of control over eating can also undermine confidence and self-esteem, reinforcing the pre-existing feeling of rejection.

The real solution does not lie in trying to fill the emotional void with food but in consciously facing the underlying feelings and identifying the triggers that lead to compulsive eating. It is essential to seek healthier ways to cope with emotional discomfort and find ways to nourish the soul without resorting to food.

Pause to Reflect

1) *Do I feel that food is one of the few sources of pleasure or comfort in my life?*

- When I feel bored or unmotivated, do I notice that eating something specific gives me a sense of reward or satisfaction?
- On days when my self-esteem is low, do I find myself turning to my favorite foods to "*treat myself*" or "*give myself a gift*"?
- Do I tend to use food to ease feelings of emptiness or lack of purpose, even when I'm not hungry?

2) *Do I feel that eating takes up a disproportionate amount of space in my thoughts or daily life?*

- Do I spend a lot of time planning my meals or anticipating what I will eat, as if food is the highlight of my day?
- Do I often worry about what I will eat before an event or specific situation, fearing that I might lose control?
- Are there situations where I feel anxious about food, such as at parties or social gatherings, because I don't know if I'll be able to resist certain foods?

3) *Do I notice that I use food as an "escape" to avoid making decisions or facing important issues?*

- When I need to make a difficult decision, do I tend to postpone it by looking for something to eat, as if food could bring clarity?

- When dealing with a conflict, do I turn to food to delay the need to face the problem or confront the person involved?
- Have I noticed that I eat compulsively when facing significant changes, such as a new phase in my career or a new relationship?
- When I have to deal with financial or health issues, do I feel the urge to eat something comforting to "*distract my mind*" and avoid discomfort?

Work Addiction

Work addiction is an escapist behavior that develops in response to the hidden wound of rejection. When we feel inadequate or incapable of meeting the expectations imposed by ourselves or others, we may turn to work as a way to seek validation and temporary relief from emotional pain. In this context, work becomes a means of filling an inner void, a way to feel useful, important, or worthy of recognition. However, this relentless pursuit of productivity and success can become a trap, leading a person to neglect other aspects of life, such as relationships, health, and leisure.

The problem with work addiction is that it is often socially accepted and even praised, making it difficult to recognize its hidden dangers. While effort and dedication are valued, work addiction goes beyond these limits, turning into compulsive behavior. The person feels incapable of stopping, even when they know they should, using work as a way to avoid or postpone dealing with difficult emotions, traumas, or conflicts. Over time, this can result in physical and emotional exhaustion, isolation, health problems, and paradoxically, a decline in professional performance—leading to even more anxiety and dissatisfaction.

Common Triggers for Work Addiction

- Fear of Failure: The anxiety of not being enough or not meeting expectations can drive a person to overwork in an attempt to avoid criticism or disapproval.
- Seeking External Validation: When self-esteem is based on recognition from others, work becomes the primary way to prove personal worth and competence.
- Guilt When Relaxing: Feeling that free time is "*wasted*" or "*unproductive*" can push someone to work constantly as a way to justify their value.
- Escaping Personal Problems: Work provides a distraction from emotional issues and problematic relationships that the person would rather not face.

Pause to Reflect

1) *Do I feel that my identity and value are directly tied to my work?*

- When I'm not producing or working, do I feel useless or without purpose?
- Do I talk more about my profession or work accomplishments than about other aspects of life, such as hobbies or relationships?

- In moments of professional success, do I feel a wave of relief and euphoria that seems to compensate for other feelings of inadequacy?
- When I meet new people, do I feel inclined to impress them with my position or professional achievements?

2) *Do I have difficulty relaxing and disconnecting from work?*

- Even on weekends or during vacations, do I feel the need to check emails or continue working on projects?
- Do I feel guilty or anxious when I take time for myself, thinking that I should be doing something productive?
- In social events or at home, does my mind frequently drift back to work-related matters, preventing me from being truly present?
- When I'm sick, do I feel compelled to work, even though I know I should rest to recover?

3) *Has work interfered with other important areas of my life?*

- Have my family or romantic relationships suffered or ended due to excessive time and dedication to work?
- Have I noticed health issues (such as insomnia, anxiety, or physical pain) that could be related to overworking?
- Have activities I used to enjoy, like hobbies or sports, been sidelined due to my workload?
- Have I ever avoided or postponed important social or personal commitments, like birthday parties or medical appointments, to prioritize work?

Smoking

Smoking is one of the most common escapist behaviors, often adopted as a defense mechanism to cope with hidden wounds of rejection. For many, smoking becomes a way to temporarily escape difficult emotions, stress, and anxieties. When a person faces rejection or criticism, the act of smoking may provide momentary relief, offering a sense of control and comfort.

Cigarettes provide a brief pause from emotional tensions but create addiction. Smoking not only impacts physical health but also perpetuates emotional rejection, as the person finds themselves trapped in a toxic relationship with the substance. This can lead to feelings of guilt and shame, resulting in more isolation and dependence on substances.

Moreover, smoking can become a way to cope with socialization and interaction with others. Some people may use smoking as a way to connect with other smokers or as an excuse to escape uncomfortable social situations. However, this practice often hides the difficulty in dealing with emotions, relationships, and self-acceptance.

Common Triggers for Smoking

- Stress and Anxiety: Pressures at work or in personal life can lead to a search for immediate relief through smoking.
- Social Rejection: Feelings of exclusion or inadequacy in social settings can trigger the desire to smoke as a way to ease emotional pain.

- Conditioned Satisfaction: The use of cigarettes can be associated with pleasurable moments, such as during a coffee break or socializing, creating an emotional connection with the act of smoking.
- Sense of Control: In moments when life feels out of control, smoking may seem like a way to regain some level of control over the situation.

Pause to Reflect

1) *Do I see smoking as a way to deal with my emotions?*

- When I feel stressed or anxious, does smoking become a way to find momentary relief?
- Do I tend to smoke more in social situations where I feel insecure or inadequate?
- Do I smoke as an automatic response to feelings of rejection or criticism, rather than directly confronting those emotions?
- Does smoking bring me a sense of comfort or security when facing conflicts or emotional challenges?

2) *Does my smoking habit interfere with my health and well-being?*

- Have I felt that my tobacco use has affected my physical health, such as difficulty breathing or heart problems?

- Have I experienced feelings of guilt or shame after smoking, especially concerning my health or the example I'm setting for others?
- Does my dependence on tobacco prevent me from participating in activities I would like to do, such as exercising or attending social events without the presence of a cigarette?
- Do I feel that smoking is negatively affecting my relationships, causing tension or misunderstandings with people who care about my health?

3) *Has smoking impacted my social life and personal relationships?*

- Have I ever avoided social gatherings or events because of my smoking habit?
- Do I find that I feel more connected to other smokers, while distancing myself from friends or family who don't smoke?
- Has smoking served as a way for me to isolate myself from social situations I find uncomfortable?
- Do I notice that the need to smoke is creating barriers in my relationships, leading to conflicts or misunderstandings?

Excessive Use of Social Media and the Internet

Excessive use of social media and the internet is an increasingly common escapist behavior, often adopted by people dealing with the hidden wound of rejection. For many, social media becomes a temporary refuge, a space where they can create an idealized image of themselves and escape the pressures and insecurities of real life. This behavior often arises as a way to cope with the emotional pain that rejection can cause.

By losing ourselves in social media, we seek validation and recognition, wishing to connect with others while distancing ourselves from real, meaningful interactions. The act of scrolling through feeds, liking posts, and engaging in online interactions can provide a sense of belonging and acceptance, even if only temporarily. However, this relief is illusory and can turn into an addiction, leading to isolation and disconnection from real life.

Excessive use of social media and the internet can also trigger constant comparisons to others' lives, increasing feelings of inadequacy and rejection. As we observe others' achievements and joys, we may feel inferior and undervalued, reinforcing the idea that we are not good enough. This perception can further fuel the need to seek validation online, leading to excessive and harmful use of these platforms.

Common Triggers for Excessive Social Media Use

- Feelings of loneliness: The lack of real social connection may lead to seeking virtual interactions as a form of compensation.
- Rejection or exclusion: Moments when we feel rejected or ignored by friends or family can intensify the desire to seek validation online.
- Low self-esteem: Difficulties with self-image can lead us to search for reaffirmation and acceptance on social media.

Pause to Reflect

1) *Do I use social media as a way to escape from my emotions?*

- When I'm feeling sad or anxious, do I find myself spending hours scrolling through social media?
- Have I noticed that I seek online distraction during moments of rejection or criticism, rather than confronting those feelings directly?
- Does liking or commenting on posts provide me with momentary relief from difficult emotions?
- Do I feel that my worth and self-esteem depend on the validation I receive on social media?

2) *Does my use of social media affect my emotional well-being?*

- Have I felt anxious or depressed after spending time on social media, especially when comparing my life to others'?
- Do I have trouble disconnecting from social media, even though I know it might be affecting my mental health?
- Does the need to always be online interfere with my ability to enjoy real-life moments and in-person interactions?
- Have I ever felt guilty about spending too much time on social media, yet continue returning to it?

3) *Does my use of social media impact my interpersonal relationships?*

- Have I ever avoided real interactions with friends or family because I was more focused on my online activities?
- Do social media interactions create misunderstandings or conflicts in my relationships due to posts or interactions that spark jealousy or insecurities?
- Do I feel that virtual interactions replace the meaningful connections I should have with the people around me?
- Do I notice that, despite having many "*friends*" online, I still feel lonely or disconnected in real life?

Self-harm and Self-destructive Behaviors

Self-harm and other self-destructive behaviors represent some of the darkest forms of escapism, often linked to the hidden wound of rejection. For those struggling with the emotional pain caused by rejection, self-harm may seem like a way to alleviate that inner pain. It is an extreme expression of despair, where the individual seeks a tangible way to manifest their emotional suffering, mistakenly believing that physical pain can offer temporary relief from psychological pain.

When a person feels rejected, devalued, or misunderstood, they may develop a connection between emotional suffering and self-harm, using cutting, burning, or other forms of self-inflicted harm as a way to externalize the pain they feel inside. This act is often preceded by intense feelings of distress, loneliness, or a sense of lack of control, making self-harm a defense mechanism, an attempt to regain control in a moment of desperation.

Additionally, self-destructive behaviors may include practices such as substance abuse, compulsive eating, or involvement in harmful relationships. Like self-harm, these behaviors are ways of coping with emotional pain, although they can create a cycle of suffering and more pain instead of offering relief.

The severity of self-harm and self-destructive behaviors should not be underestimated. These behaviors often become a form of silent communication, where the person struggles to express their pain and needs in a way that is visible to others. Self-harm can be a desperate attempt to seek attention or help, although paradoxically, it may also push away those who care the most.

Common Triggers for Self-harm and Self-destructive Behaviors

- Moments of intense rejection or criticism, whether in personal or professional relationships, can trigger these behaviors.
- The feeling of being alone in the world, without emotional support, can lead to self-destructive behaviors as a way of coping with the pain.
- Situations that generate intense emotional despair, such as the loss of a loved one or a breakup, may trigger self-harm as a form of expression.
- Difficulties in accepting oneself and feelings of inadequacy can lead to behaviors that harm one's physical and emotional health.

Pause to Reflect

1) *Do I see myself using self-harm as a way to cope with my emotions?*

- In moments of emotional crisis, have I physically harmed myself as a way to relieve my pain?
- Do I feel that self-harm provides temporary relief, but then emotional pain returns even more intensely?
- When I feel rejected or criticized, do I tend to hurt myself as a way to express my suffering?

2) *Do my self-destructive behaviors affect my overall well-being?*

- Have I ever felt trapped in a cycle of behaviors that, while providing temporary relief, result in more pain and regret?
- Do my self-destructive behaviors interfere with my personal relationships, causing distance from those who care about me?
- Do I feel that by engaging in self-destructive behaviors, I am losing control over my life and decisions?

3) *Do self-harm or self-destructive behaviors impact my interpersonal relationships?*

- Have I ever felt unable to share my emotional struggles with friends or family, leading to an increase in self-harm as a way of coping with the pain?
- Does the need to hide my self-destructive behaviors make me feel even more isolated and misunderstood?
- Have I noticed that self-harm affects my ability to connect emotionally with others?
- Do the people around me show concern for me, but I feel unable to open up about what I'm really going through?

Compulsive Shopping

Compulsive shopping emerges as one of the most common escapist behaviors among those struggling with the hidden wound of rejection. For many people, shopping becomes a temporary escape from emotional pain, serving as a way to alleviate psychological discomfort and feelings of inadequacy. Purchasing new items can create a fleeting sense of euphoria, providing a temporary feeling of control and satisfaction. However, this sensation is often short-lived and followed by a cycle of guilt and regret, which can intensify the underlying emotional distress.

A person suffering from feelings of rejection may seek to fill an emotional void through excessive consumption. Shopping becomes a defense mechanism, where each purchase is seen as an attempt to compensate for the lack of validation and love they feel. For example, someone might feel lonely and, instead of confronting that pain, choose to go shopping, believing that a new outfit, trinket, or home décor item will bring happiness and fulfillment. This endless pursuit of external validation through material possessions can quickly turn into an addiction, where momentary pleasure is followed by dissatisfaction and the urge to shop again.

Moreover, shopping can also serve as a disguise for deeper emotions, such as sadness, anger, or frustration. When these emotions are ignored or suppressed, compulsive shopping becomes a way to avoid facing real issues. This form of escapism, though seemingly harmless at first, can cause serious financial and emotional harm, leading to cycles of debt, stress, and dissatisfaction.

Common Triggers for Compulsive Shopping

- Feeling inferior or undervalued may lead a person to shop as a way to temporarily boost self-esteem.
- Loneliness can trigger shopping as an attempt to fill an emotional void.
- High emotional pressure, such as work or relationship problems, can spark the urge to shop as a way to relieve tension.
- Social pressure to stay trendy or own the latest products can lead to impulsive purchases in an attempt to feel accepted and valued.

Pause to Reflect

1) *Do I Use Shopping as a Way to Cope with My Emotions?*

- When I feel sad or discouraged, do I tend to shop as a way to feel better?
- Have I noticed that after a negative experience, I tend to go shopping to "*compensate*" for the emotional pain I am feeling?
- Does shopping temporarily relieve my anxiety, only to be followed by guilt over spending money?
- Have I ever caught myself buying things I don't need just to distract myself or forget my problems?

2) *Do My Shopping Habits Impact My Financial and Emotional Well-Being?*

- Have I noticed that my frequent shopping is leading to financial difficulties, such as debt or economic stress?
- Do I feel that my shopping habits interfere with other areas of my life, such as relationships and financial responsibilities?
- After making a purchase, do I feel satisfied for a brief moment, only to quickly return to feeling dissatisfied and wanting to buy more?
- Have I ever felt overwhelmed by the amount of items I've acquired but don't use, resulting in feelings of frustration and regret?

3) *Do Compulsive Shopping Habits Affect My Relationships?*

- Have I noticed that my excessive spending causes concern among friends and family?
- Does the need to hide my purchases or lie about my spending create tension in my relationships?
- Do I feel unable to open up to those close to me about my struggles with compulsive shopping?
- Does the feeling that I need to shop to feel accepted or loved negatively impact my relationships?

As I've mentioned before, in the early years of my marriage, my income was not enough to cover our expenses. Instead of facing this problem head-on and seeking a stable financial solution, I chose the path of escape. I took refuge in excessive spending, trying to compensate for my pain and my constant need for validation. In my mind, living in a good and comfortable home would be a way to mask my inertia in the face of the daily struggles that affected my family.

However, the rent for these houses always exceeded my financial capacity. This led to constant delays in paying rent, water, and electricity bills, creating a cycle of embarrassment and suffering. My family became dependent on financial help from my wife's relatives, which only deepened my frustration and sense of inadequacy. The more frustrated I felt, the stronger my need for validation became—and the bigger the house I rented, perpetuating this painful and unsustainable cycle.

After decades of living in this pattern, when we finally managed to overcome our financial instability, instead of feeling relieved, I realized that my deep-seated rejection wound—rooted in my relentless search for validation—had reached its peak. When I started earning a more stable income and could provide some security for my family, I developed the belief that my only real value was in my work.

This belief turned into a new destructive cycle. My emotional reactivity reached alarming levels. Every time my wife tried to get closer or reminded me to give more attention to our relationship, I would explode. I couldn't handle the pain of my rejection wound, now compounded by the dynamics created by my constant need for validation and approval. So, I buried myself even deeper in my work, using it as a refuge. There, I felt valued and recognized, while escaping from the reality and the pain that awaited me at home.

Rejection, when left unidentified and unaddressed, can shape not only our choices but also our most important relationships in a destructive way. It is a cycle that feeds on pain and blinds us to the impact our actions have on ourselves and the people we love.

Here we arrive at the end of another stage in this journey of self-awareness. I hope that, like me, you have experienced a sense of self-discovery—that you have been able to explore the deepest corners of your subconscious and bring to light feelings that have remained hidden for a long time. Now that these feelings have been exposed to the light of awareness, they are ready for an update.

After all, years have passed, many things have changed, and new tools have been incorporated into your life. The time has come to adjust and align these feelings and behaviors with your current reality.

By becoming aware of these patterns, you recognize that they do not define your identity; rather, they are simply side effects of a hidden rejection wound. More important than just identifying these behaviors is understanding that they can be reprogrammed.

Now, you are ready for a crucial step: taking responsibility to act, confronting the patterns that have shaped your life until now, and transforming your reactions and choices. True change only happens when you take the initiative to shift these behaviors.

12

THE FIRST STEP TOWARD TRANSFORMATION

Up to this point, we have explored how the hidden wound of rejection shapes many of our behaviors—behaviors that, without realizing it, have been limiting our lives. Now that we are aware of this, it is up to us to decide what we will do with this knowledge. Awareness is only the first step in a long journey. The next step—more challenging, but also more rewarding—is to take action.

Every dysfunctional behavior we have identified throughout the previous chapters was built as a response to painful experiences that we interpreted as rejection. These automatic responses were created at a time when we lacked the emotional resources to cope with the pain of rejection. Now, however, we have the opportunity to act differently. We can restructure these behaviors and, in doing so, reprogram our brains.

If in the past we reacted automatically to certain triggers, we can now choose new responses. This, however, requires effort and commitment. Reprogramming the brain to stop activating these "*defense routines*" in response to rejection triggers demands constant work, but the benefits are immeasurable.

Reprogramming

The Path to Unlocking Your Potential

In the next section of this book, we will explore specific tools and techniques to reprogram these behaviors. We will learn how to identify the origins of the emotions that triggered such reactions and find new ways to respond. As we already know, the brain is adaptable, capable of creating new connections—new neural "*routines.*" This means that by intentionally repeating new behaviors, we can strengthen these new pathways and gradually weaken the old patterns that have been holding us back.

For example, if the fear of failure prevents us from taking action toward our goals, we will learn how to deactivate that fear. Instead of allowing it to paralyze us, we can reshape our perception of failure. We can learn to see failure not as confirmation of our inadequacy, but as an opportunity for growth. By doing this repeatedly, we create a new neural response—a new pathway that activates in moments of challenge.

This reprogramming applies not only to behaviors in our personal lives but also to our professional lives, our relationships, and our creative expression. Think of all the limitations we have addressed in different areas of our lives throughout the previous chapters. All of these behaviors can be restructured. We can create new responses that allow us to act with confidence, clarity, and authenticity.

Breaking the Curse of Rejection

Perhaps one of the most important aspects of this reprogramming journey is the opportunity to break a generational cycle of rejection. Many of the limiting behaviors we exhibit today are the result of emotional patterns inherited from our parents, who, in turn, inherited them from their own parents. This repetitive cycle is passed down from generation to generation, as children absorb the emotional environment of their caregivers and internalize the same fears, insecurities, and defense mechanisms.

For example, if our parents dealt with feelings of rejection by being overly critical of themselves or others, we likely learned to do the same. If they avoided conflict or suppressed their emotions, we may have adopted these defense strategies as well. And so, we continue perpetuating this "*curse*" for future generations. However, now that we are aware of these patterns, we have the power to interrupt them. By reprogramming our behaviors, we are not only healing ourselves; we are also preventing our children and grandchildren from inheriting the same fears and insecurities.

The impact of this transformation is profound. We do not just free ourselves—we also give future generations the opportunity to live free from these limiting patterns. Our choice to change today can break the cycle of rejection that has persisted for generations in our family, setting us free and allowing our descendants to live a more authentic, fulfilling, and meaningful life.

The Opportunity to Unlock Life

When we decide to reprogram our behaviors, we open the doors to a new world of possibilities. Every pattern we identify and overcome brings us closer to a lighter, freer life, more in tune with who we truly are. Every limiting behavior we leave behind is an opportunity to unlock our life, our abilities, and our true potential.

The "*routines*" of rejection create a narrow and distorted view of our capabilities. By reprogramming these behaviors, we begin to see life differently. We start believing in ourselves more, trusting our abilities, and allowing ourselves to explore our full potential.

Transformation does not happen overnight. It requires practice, patience, and dedication. But over time, we begin to see the results. We start feeling more confident, less reactive, and more at peace with who we are. Our relationships improve, our productivity increases, and we begin to experience a sense of fulfillment that once seemed unattainable.

The Choice to Change

Throughout this book, you have explored how wounds of rejection can impact every aspect of your life. From your self-esteem to your relationships, your creative expression to your professional success, these limiting behaviors may have prevented you from fully living. But now, with the knowledge you have gained, it is time to make an important choice: the choice to change.

You are at a crucial turning point in your journey. You can continue being held captive by these patterns, allowing them to control your reactions, sabotage your plans, and limit your true potential, or you can make the conscious decision to reprogram them. It may not seem easy, but this is one of the most powerful decisions you can make for yourself. Choosing to change is choosing freedom. It is embracing the opportunity to rewrite your life story, leaving behind the habits that hold you back and adopting new ways of being that will lead you to success, happiness, and fulfillment.

This choice will not only transform your own life but will also have a profound impact on those around you—especially your children, grandchildren, and everyone who interacts with you. When you choose to grow and heal, you create a ripple effect that can change generations. Think about the power of your decision: you have the ability to be the link that breaks the cycle of limiting patterns inherited over the years, allowing future generations to live free from these conditionings. What you decide now will echo beyond yourself.

In the next part of this book, you will find the tools and techniques to help you achieve this transformation. They will guide you through every step of mental and emotional reprogramming. You will learn to identify the origins of the feelings that have triggered these behaviors throughout your life and how to reprogram your automatic responses to these triggers. Imagine the freedom that will come when, instead of impulsively reacting to situations that once caused pain and frustration, you can choose a conscious and healthy response. It will be a journey of self-discovery and healing, a process that will allow you to unleash your full potential and start living life with more authenticity, freedom, and joy.

Now, with the knowledge you have, the responsibility is yours. You have the chance to transform your life. No matter how deeply ingrained old patterns may be or how long limiting beliefs have been part of your story—you can change. You are not destined to repeat the past or remain trapped in the same emotional pitfalls. Science shows us that the brain is adaptable, and with the right effort, you can create new neural connections, new emotional responses, and new behaviors that will lead you to a much more fulfilling life.

Think about the inspiration you will be to others by proving that it is possible to change, grow, and overcome emotional obstacles that once seemed insurmountable. By choosing to transform your behaviors, you are investing in the future of your life and the future of those you love.

In this next phase, trust the process. Yes, there will be difficult moments, but there will also be moments of great revelation and personal victory. The reprogramming journey you are about to embark on will be a milestone in your life, a turning point that will lead you to a new chapter of growth, fulfillment, and inner peace.

So, embrace this journey with courage and determination. The full and meaningful life you desire is within your reach. There are no more excuses, no turning back. The knowledge is here, the path is before you, and now it is up to you to take the next step. May the motivation to unleash your full potential and live your life with purpose guide you forward, and may the certainty that this journey is worth every effort inspire you to persist until you achieve the transformation you so deeply desire.

This is your moment.

PART II

Masters Are Those Who Teach Themselves!

13

SELF-AWARENESS

As we explore the main groups of defense mechanisms and the escapist behaviors that the hidden wound of rejection develops throughout our lives, we begin to see how these behaviors—whether compulsions, addictions, or self-destructive actions—serve as disguises, masking a deep and silent pain: the feeling of not being accepted or valued.

Through the descriptions and reflection exercises, we had the opportunity to examine our behaviors, feelings, actions, and daily reactions, searching for signs that the hidden wound of rejection has been present, shaping our choices and influencing our relationships. By analyzing our attitudes in depth, we can identify which patterns dominate our lives and how these defense mechanisms may be operating as automatic responses to unresolved emotional pain.

The investigative process we have undertaken so far has provided us with valuable clues. By analyzing the predominant group of behaviors in our decisions and reactions, we can begin to see how the wound of rejection may have originated at some point in the past. This wound may have manifested in various ways—through an episode of social exclusion, constant criticism, emotional neglect, or other traumatic experiences. The impact of this initial event left marks on our emotional development, and as we encountered similar situations over time, this pattern continued to repeat itself, reinforcing a cycle that traps us and distances us from our true essence.

Now, it is time to go further. In the following chapters, we will delve deeper into the search for the events that gave rise to the wound of rejection. These situations, often forgotten or repressed, were interpreted by our brain as rejection and have since shaped the way we perceive the world and interact with others. It is essential that we face these events with courage and compassion, for it is through this deep understanding that we will finally be able to break free from the chains of this hidden wound.

By identifying the origins of the wound of rejection, we will be able to give new meaning to these experiences, rewriting the narrative of pain and suffering that has conditioned us for so long. This process of reframing is an opportunity to reclaim our emotional freedom and reprogram the automatic patterns that have led us down unwanted paths—paths we no longer wish to follow.

Each identified event will be a step toward freedom, a release from the "*routines*" that have unconsciously directed our lives. We will finally take control, redirecting our destiny toward places that bring us fulfillment, wholeness, and the possibility of becoming the best version of ourselves. Together, step by step, we will untie the knots that have prevented us from living authentically and reconnect with our truest essence.

Time to Take Action

By practicing the reflection exercises proposed for each behavior described in the previous chapters, you have already taken a significant step on your journey of change. The simple realization that some behaviors—ones you previously believed to be integral parts of your personality—are actually reflections of the hidden wound of rejection has already begun to break some of the chains that once held you captive. This initial understanding has brought a fresh perspective, allowing you to see your life and relationships in a new light.

Now, a spark of optimism is beginning to emerge within you, and along with it, a growing desire to explore more deeply what lies hidden in your inner world. As you uncover these patterns, a door opens to a path of healing and transformation, and each step forward is an invitation to continue breaking the chains that still remain.

The next step in this journey is to identify the original event that triggered the hidden wound of rejection. The exercises you have completed will help you rank, from 1 to 10, the behaviors you resonate with the most. Now, it is time to organize them, ranking them in order of intensity. This process of categorization will reveal the group of behaviors that is most dominant in your life and will serve as a compass to guide you in identifying specific moments from your past that gave rise to the wound of rejection. These correlations are essential for tracing the path back to the primary event, allowing you to locate it and clearly understand the impact it has had on your life.

Let's revisit the correlations between behavior patterns and the possible events that may have triggered the wound of rejection. This analysis will serve as a starting point for identifying the key experiences that conditioned you and influenced your choices, helping you understand how these behaviors became a way of coping with pain and the fear of rejection. From this point forward, we will move toward uncovering the pivotal events and, through this understanding, begin to free your mind and heart from the "*routines*" that have been guiding your life on autopilot.

Rate from 01 to 10 the behaviors you have identified as the most dominant in your life.

Self-Image and Self-Esteem

Behavior	**Cause**	**(1-10)**
Low self-esteem	*Comparisons or devaluation*	( )
Excessive self-criticism	*Constant criticism*	( )
Impostor syndrome	*Lack of recognition*	( )
Personal shame	*Shame or public humiliation*	( )

Need for Control and Security

Behavior	**Cause**	**(1-10)**
Obsessive behavior and excessive control	*Family instability*	( )
Perfectionism	*Constant criticism*	( )
Exaggerated self-sufficiency	*Lack of support*	( )
Inflexibility	*Family instability*	( )

Ability to Relate to Others

Behavior	**Cause**	**(1-10)**
Social anxiety	*Public humiliation*	( )
Fear of intimacy	*Emotional abandonment*	( )
Emotional dependency	*Lack of affection*	( )
Conflict avoidance	*Family devaluation*	( )
Need for approval	*Social exclusion*	( )
Isolation	*Constant rejection by groups*	( )

Procrastination and Performance

Behavior	**Cause**	**(1-10)**
Chronic procrastination	*Lack of validation*	( )
Premature abandonment	*Repeated failures*	( )
Underachievement	*Academic devaluation*	( )
Fear of failure	*High expectations*	( )
Self-sabotage	*Excessive expectations*	( )

Emotional Reactivity

Behavior	**Cause**	**(1-10)**
Excessive reactivity	*Aggressive criticism*	( )
Emotional instability	*Abandonment*	( )
Defensive behavior	*Devaluation*	( )
Constant irritability	*Negative comparisons*	( )
Outbursts of anger	*Frequent conflicts*	( )

Distrust and Toxic Relationships

Behavior	**Cause**	**(1-10)**
Excessive distrust	*Broken promises*	( )
Pathological jealousy	*Emotional betrayals*	( )
Tendency toward abusive relationships	*Psychological violence*	( )
Relational paranoia	*Abandonment*	( )
Attraction to destructive relationships	*Disrespect*	( )

Self-Expression and Creativity

Behavior	**Cause**	**(1-10)**
Creative block	*Criticism of creative expression*	( )
Fear of self-expression	*Family disapproval*	( )
Talent inhibition	*Lack of encouragement*	( )
Conformity	*Not meeting expectations*	( )
Artistic insecurity	*Criticism of arts or skills*	( )

Now that you've assessed how much you identify with each item, it's time to understand how these scores can help you pinpoint the specific areas of your life where the hidden wound of rejection has had the greatest impact.

Follow the steps below to interpret your results:

1. *Add up the scores for each group of behaviors.*
   Each group represents an area of your life (such as self-esteem, relationships, or creativity). By summing up the points for each group, you'll see which area has been most affected by rejection.

2. *Identify the group with the highest score.*
   The group with the highest score reveals the behaviors where the hidden wound of rejection is exerting the greatest influence on your life. This group indicates the area that requires the most attention and care.
3. *Analyze the highest-scoring behaviors within that group.*
   Within the group with the highest score, take note of which specific behaviors received the highest ratings. These behaviors will help you identify the root cause of your hidden wound of rejection.

   Example: If the highest-rated behavior is Emotional Outbursts, then your originating event may be related to abandonment or a lack of emotional support. Once you've identified the most likely cause of your hidden wound of rejection, it's time to move on to the next steps...

Identifying the Origins of theHidden Wound of Rejection

Using these correlations as a guide, it becomes easier to search through the archives of our memories for the event that left the deepest emotional mark. Sometimes, we are already aware of these events but fail to recognize just how profound and impactful they were, or how the rejection they caused left lasting scars.

This happens because we tend to remember events as concrete facts—simple occurrences—without realizing the emotional weight they carried. And it is precisely in these cases that the hidden wound of rejection takes hold: we know objectively what happened, but we overlook the deep effects that experience had on our lives.

My Hidden Wound of Rejection

I have always held a vivid memory of the day my father called me to help him wash the car. When I said I didn't want to, he responded by spraying me with cold water from the hose, drenching me completely.

For a long time, I carried this memory as an example of how children should obey their parents and respect their wishes. However, during a period of my life when I felt stuck, unable to reach the potential I believed I had, I decided to speak with a psychologist. He suggested that I look for answers in my childhood, and that memory of the "*hose bath*" resurfaced. This time, it came with a sense of resentment. But I dismissed it, thinking, *Come on, it was just water—why make such a big deal out of it?* At the time, reflecting on it superficially wasn't enough to change anything, and I continued living the same way.

It was only recently, when I truly committed to finding the root of what was holding me back from living fully, that I revisited this event with deeper awareness. Using meditation and self-reflection techniques—ones I will share in the next chapter—I was able to go back to that moment and feel the emotions that had been buried. For the first time, I recognized the birth of the hidden wound of rejection that had shaped my life for over forty years.

At the time, I lived with my paternal grandparents on a farm in a small countryside town. There was no electricity or running water; nights were lit only by the moon, the stars, and kerosene lamps. The nearest drinking water came from a small stream about 500 meters from the house, and to get to town—three kilometers away—we had to walk or, on rare occasions, ride a horse.

My father lived in a neighboring town with my stepmother and half-sister. On weekends, he would visit us, and on one of these visits, he took me to spend a few days at his house. The contrast between the two worlds was enormous: his house was in the city, with electricity, running water, a bathroom, and a hot shower. The floors were polished to a shine, their waxy scent lingering in the air, and the windows had glass panes with curtains—a true luxury for someone who had never experienced such comforts. I was both fascinated and jealous of the life my half-sister had there.

One afternoon, my stepmother asked me to take a bath because my father would be home from work soon. When I finished, he was already in the garage, washing the car. I ran to see him, and from the doorway, I could see him down below, focused on his work. When he spotted me, he called me over to help, but I told him I couldn't—I had just taken a bath.

His reaction was immediate: he raised the hose and drenched me completely. I ran off crying, overwhelmed by a deep pain I couldn't understand.

At that moment, the sense of not belonging, which had already been creeping in since I arrived at his house, became unbearable. Seeing my sister's life, experiencing that new reality, only reinforced the feeling that I didn't belong. And now, my father's action seemed to confirm it: I wasn't good enough.

How could he love me if I couldn't even help him wash the car just because I wanted to keep my clothes clean? And the worst part? My clothes were wet and dirty anyway—I would have to bathe again. Why had I disobeyed my father in my first opportunity to be with him?

During those days, my stepmother would ask if I was enjoying my time there and whether I wanted to live with them. Of course, I did—to me, it would have been a dream. One evening, during dinner, she casually mentioned to my father, "*Gerson said he'd like to come live with us.*"

His response was immediate and firm:

"*No. His place is with my mother—he is well taken care of there.*"

Revisiting this memory made me realize that, until that moment, I had never experienced anything that triggered such a deep feeling of rejection. That was the origin—the starting point of the hidden wound of rejection that would shape my actions and beliefs for decades. From that moment on, my brain developed "*routines*" that remained in a constant state of alert, always scanning for any sign of rejection, no matter how small.

Next, I will introduce the technique I used to guide my awareness back to that moment and retrieve all the insights I have just shared.

14

MEDITATION AND REFLECTION TECHNIQUE

The goal here is to create an environment for introspection and self-exploration, allowing you to revisit every event that, at some point, you may have interpreted as rejection. The objective is to return to these moments and consciously relive them, no matter how painful it may be. Simply recalling an event is not enough; in most cases, remembering that something happened is merely acknowledging its occurrence. At this stage of the healing process, it is necessary to revisit the experience as if embarking on a "*time journey*," placing yourself in the role of an observer visiting the event so that you can see all the elements involved from a new perspective.

Likewise, it is essential to ask the suggested questions in this technique during meditation to sharpen your senses. Our brain operates through associations—music can transport us to a specific memory, a scent can bring back a past experience. Our defense mechanisms tend to obscure details of painful events to protect us from reliving the pain each time the memory arises.

For example, in my case, I only remembered the hose bath, but I had no recollection of the conversation at the dinner table. My brain, recognizing that this was the most painful part associated with the feeling of rejection, kept it hidden. However, by using this technique, I was able to sharpen my senses and recall the details of the house's interior: the bedrooms, the TV room, the color of the floor, the scent of wax—and then, the memory of the conversation surfaced.

Initial Preparation

Find a quiet place where you won't be interrupted. Sit or lie down in a comfortable position. Close your eyes and take a few deep breaths, allowing your body to relax with each exhalation.

Focus on your breathing. Inhale slowly and deeply, filling your lungs, then exhale gently, releasing any tension. Repeat this for a few minutes until you feel calmer and more centered.

Visualize a time machine. Use your imagination—it could be the *DeLorean* from Back to the Future or any other kind of machine that represents time travel for you. Picture yourself stepping inside and setting the coordinates for a specific moment in your past.

Choose an event to revisit. Using the behavior and its underlying cause that you identified most strongly in the previous chapter as a guide, think of a moment in your life when you experienced a deep sense of rejection, even if it's just a vague or seemingly insignificant memory. Set the time machine to the exact day or an approximate period when this event occurred.

Arriving at the past moment. Imagine stepping out of the time machine and arriving precisely at the instant when the event took place. See your younger self going through that situation.

Observe the Environment Around You Carefully

What does the setting look like? Are you indoors or outdoors?

If indoors: What kind of place is it? A house, a school, a workplace, or somewhere else? Are there familiar objects around you? How are they arranged?

If outdoors: Are you in a park, on the street, in the countryside? Are there trees, buildings, or other structures nearby? What is the space like—open, cramped, chaotic, or organized?

What is the weather like? Is it warm, cold, rainy, or sunny?

If warm: Is the heat comfortable or uncomfortable?

If cold: How does the cold affect you? Is it snowing, windy, or just chilly?

If rainy: Is it a light drizzle or a heavy downpour? Are you sheltered or getting wet?

What time of day is it? Is it bright or dark? Is it morning, afternoon, or night?

If it's bright: Is the light intense or soft? Does it come from the sun, lamps, or other sources?

If it's dark: Can you see anything? Are there lights around, such as streetlights or candles?

What is the air like around you? Feel the temperature and notice the smells. You might pick up the scent of an object, a plant, or even the atmosphere of the place.

Is the air humid or dry Is there a specific aroma, such as food, perfume, nature, or chemicals? Is the smell pleasant or unpleasant?

Take a deep breath and observe if there's anything in the air that triggers a particular sensation. Does it evoke another memory or emotion?

Your younger self is present. Observe this version of yourself closely:

What is your younger self wearing? What kind of clothes does this version of yourself have on? Are you in school clothes, work attire, or something casual? Are you barefoot or wearing shoes?

What is your posture like? Are you standing, sitting, or lying down? Is your posture relaxed or tense?

Who is with you? Are you alone or in the company of others? If there are other people, who are they—family, friends, colleagues, or strangers? How are they reacting to what is happening?

What is happening around you? Is it a conversation, an argument, a game, a conflict, or a celebration? How is this version of yourself reacting? Are you silent, crying, yelling, laughing, or staying quiet?

Explore Your Younger Self's Emotions

How are you feeling? Sad, scared, confused, angry, or ashamed? Try to identify the primary emotion and any other feelings that may be present.

How do these emotions manifest in your body? Are you trembling, feeling your heart race, breathing rapidly, or experiencing a knot in your stomach?

Look at the context around you

What else is happening in the environment? Is there any situation or event in the background that might be affecting your younger self, even if indirectly?

Are there sounds in the background? Such as voices, music, traffic noise, or other sounds? Are they increasing the feeling of rejection or providing comfort?

Is there something your younger self wishes to do or say at that moment but cannot? What is the reason your younger self feels unable to act or express?

Examine your younger self's facial expression and body

What is your expression like? Wide eyes, furrowed brows, trembling lips? Do these expressions convey specific emotions?

Observe if your younger self is hiding or trying to distance himself or herself from something or someone. Is there any part of the body he or she seems to be protecting, like crossed arms or a hidden face?

Look for any signs of hope or comfort

Even if the pain is intense, is there any element around that brings a sense of safety or hope? Perhaps a friendly person, a familiar object, or just a corner where your younger self can feel a little safer?

Relive the emotions

Observe your younger self

See how he or she is reacting. What emotions are emerging?

Do you feel sad, angry, scared, or confused? Allow yourself to feel these emotions deeply, without judging or repressing them.

Compare with the current pain

Ask yourself: Is this pain similar to what I feel today?

Are the defensive and escape behaviors I've adopted currently trying to avoid the same pain?

Look for previous events

If you feel this pain has appeared before in your life, go back to the time machine and adjust the coordinates to an earlier event where this feeling may have originated. Keep doing this until you find the original event, the first time this feeling emerged.

Deepening and Understanding

Stay with the deepest event you've found. Now, deepen your analysis:

- How old were you? What did you look like physically?

- What were your expectations or dreams at that time?

What did you believe would happen, and what actually happened?

- How did the environment and the people around you contribute to the wound of rejection?

Look with compassion

Look at your younger self with empathy and understanding. See how hard he or she tried to cope with that pain, even without knowing how. Understand that the defenses and strategies he or she created were a form of emotional survival.

Return to the present

Go back to the time machine. Thank the opportunity to have revisited this moment and to have brought a new understanding to the present. Adjust the coordinates to the present time and return to your body, here and now.

Take a few deep breaths. Feel the air entering and leaving your lungs, and slowly begin to move your fingers and toes. Open your eyes when you feel ready.

Post-Meditation Reflection

Take a notebook and write about the experience. Note the details of the event, the emotions felt, and any new insights that emerged. Ask yourself: What have I learned about myself? How can I use this understanding to begin healing this wound of rejection?

Closure

Allow yourself time to process. After such a deep experience, give yourself the space needed to process the emotions. If you feel the need, repeat the technique on other occasions to explore new events or dive even deeper into this journey of self-discovery.

It may be necessary to repeat the technique until you reach a satisfying result—identifying the event that gave rise to the hidden wound of rejection. For those who are not accustomed to meditating or deeply reflecting on certain topics, the process may feel more challenging at first. However, with time and as the practice is repeated, it will become easier to relax and focus on the goal.

Practice the technique until you can identify the specific event in your life and relive it without fear or judgment, closely observing every detail. Not all details may surface during the meditation exercise, but they can emerge spontaneously at later moments, such as when waking up, taking a shower, or watching TV. Once the brain is triggered to investigate the event through the suggested technique, it will continue searching through memory archives, gradually bringing those memories to the surface.

Keep a journal of your practices, noting everything that has been remembered, felt, and discovered. The act of writing enhances your focus on the subject and makes your brain more active, helping in the search.

Once you identify the event that originated the hidden wound of rejection, you will be ready to move on to the next step.

15

FRAMING

Framing is a psychological strategy used to alter the way we interpret or perceive a situation. It involves changing the "*frame*" or context in which an experience is viewed, which can modify the meaning we assign to it. By adjusting our perspective, we can transform how we feel about an event, behavior, or thought, generating new interpretations that promote a more positive or functional outlook.

For example, an experience of rejection might initially be interpreted negatively, leading to feelings of inadequacy or worthlessness. However, through framing, we can reassess the event as an opportunity to develop resilience and self-awareness. In this new "*frame*," rejection is no longer seen merely as proof that we are not enough, but rather as an experience that can teach us to set healthier boundaries, value ourselves, and seek more authentic connections. This type of reframing allows us to access the "*routine*" of the defense mechanisms created by the original event and reprogram them, significantly altering their patterns.

Framing is a powerful tool for reinterpreting and redefining events, enabling us to see challenges from new perspectives. It helps us shift the context of an event, transforming what seems like a flaw into a strength, depending on the circumstances. For instance, a behavior that may be perceived as stubbornness in one situation could be seen as determination in a scenario that requires persistence. Additionally, framing allows us to redefine the meaning of an experience without altering the facts. A mistake, rather than being viewed as a failure, can be valued as an important lesson for growth.

Another application of framing is the ability to focus on hidden benefits within negative experiences. Losing a job, for example, can be seen as an opportunity to redirect one's career or explore new paths that align more closely with one's values. Finally, framing also encourages us to reassess events with the perspective of time, helping us realize that what seems like a major problem today may become irrelevant or even beneficial in the future. With this shift in perception, we become capable of finding growth and purpose even in adversity.

Framing is widely used in cognitive-behavioral therapies because it helps individuals recognize and restructure thought patterns that cause distress. When practiced regularly, this strategy can contribute to developing a more resilient mindset, one that is better equipped to handle challenges in a balanced and effective way.

Consciously framing thoughts and situations allows us to take a more proactive approach to problems and train our minds to see the positive aspects or growth opportunities in adverse situations. That is why framing is such a powerful technique for fostering changes in behavior and emotions, ultimately helping to build a lighter, more fulfilling life.

When I identified the event that triggered my hidden wound of rejection—using the reflection technique mentioned earlier—I was able to analyze it from the perspective of my adult self, equipped with the tools and knowledge I possess today. This distance allowed me to stop seeing it solely through the limited lens of the four-year-old child I was at the time. By applying the framing technique to the event, I was able to redefine the experience and completely transform the emotions previously associated with it.

In my process of framing the event, I began to reconsider the context of the "*hose bath*." What if, instead of being an act of disapproval for refusing to help wash the car, my father—through an awkward attempt at playfulness or connection—simply wanted to share a fun moment with me? However, due to a lack of sensitivity or understanding of my feelings, his action was interpreted negatively. In this new context, I started to see the event as an attempt at bonding that was misunderstood by both of us, rather than as direct rejection.

My feelings of not belonging and being rejected may have been a natural reaction to a significant contrast in environments. The transition from a simple life on the farm to a house in the city—with certain luxuries and a half-sister who was already adapted to that reality—created a challenge that any child might struggle to navigate. Under this new perspective, the "*hose bath*" was no longer the central event but merely a trigger for an already latent sense of inadequacy. This feeling did not stem from a single situation but was the result of complex circumstances, including the fact that I had been separated from my mother at just one year old. It was not necessarily a lack of love or acceptance from my father, but rather a convergence of events that deeply shaped my sense of belonging.

Seeing the event in retrospect, I realized that the pain I felt at four years old was amplified by how I processed the situation and how I interpreted my father's actions. When revisiting the memory as an adult, I could recognize that my father had no intention of causing harm. His behavior may have been a result of a lack of empathy and ineffective communication, but not necessarily a conscious desire to reject me as his son. Looking at the event with temporal distance helped reduce the emotional weight and allowed me to see the situation in a more balanced way.

After these reflections, I was able to fully reframe the event. The following is my new perspective on it.

New Version of the Event

At that time, I lived with my paternal grandparents on a farm in a small countryside town. The simplicity of the place had a certain charm: the nights were illuminated by the light of the moon and the stars, and water was collected from a nearby stream. To get to town, we walked 3 km or, sometimes, rode a horse.

When my father took me to spend a few days at his house, the contrast between the farm and city life surprised me. He lived with my stepmother and my half-sister in a house that seemed like another world to me: it had electricity, running water, and even an electric shower. The polished wooden floor gleamed, and there were curtains on the glass windows. It was a fascinating environment, but it also stirred a mix of admiration and jealousy in me regarding the life my sister had there. I didn't fully understand what I was feeling at the time, but now I realize that I was discovering a new reality, and with it came questions about my own place in the world.

I remember one afternoon when my stepmother asked me to take a bath because my father would be home from work soon. I got out of the bath and ran to see him in the garage, where he was washing the car. When he saw me, he called me over to help. At that moment, I hesitated. My childish mind associated bathing with a long and laborious process (on the farm, bathing involved going to the stream, fetching water, heating it on the wood stove, and mixing it with cold water in a basin—it wasn't just a matter of stepping into the bathroom and turning on the shower). I was clean, just as my stepmother had asked, and helping wash the car could ruin that. So I told him I couldn't because I had just bathed and was wearing clean clothes.

He responded by lifting the hose and soaking me completely. In that instant, a deep pain took hold of me. I used to interpret it as rejection, as if he were pushing me away. However, now, revisiting this memory with a new perspective, I realize that my father was probably trying to include me in his routine in a playful way—perhaps without realizing how it might affect me.

The feeling of not belonging that I already carried was amplified by the context: I was discovering a different life and, deep down, I wanted to be part of it. Looking back now, I see that I interpreted my father's reaction negatively because I already had a deep-seated fear—the fear of not being accepted. When my stepmother mentioned at dinner that I wanted to live with them, my father's firm response, saying that my place was with my grandmother, felt like rejection to me. But now, reframing this scene, I understand that he was actually protecting me. In his view, I was already well cared for and loved by my grandparents, and his relationship with my stepmother was already strained—they separated shortly afterward. He wanted to maintain the stability of my life rather than bring about changes that certainly wouldn't have been better for me.

Today, with a new perspective, I can see that what once felt like rejection was actually an attempt at care and a reflection of my father's emotional limitations. He wasn't perfect, just as none of us are, but there was no lack of love. I simply wasn't able to recognize it at the time. Understanding this has allowed me to release the weight of that memory and see that, even in the midst of my childhood emotional confusion, there was love and concern—just expressed in a way I couldn't comprehend at the time.

To understand how the hidden wound of rejection shapes our lives, it takes more than just knowing the facts. In my case, even knowing that my father separated from my stepmother shortly after that event, the wound of rejection born in that moment continued to operate and solidify over the years. It fed on every new situation that, in some way, reminded me of rejection, shaping my choices and my perception of myself.

We need to go further. We must revisit the event, analyze it in the context in which it occurred, and then view it from the perspective of our present self—a version of us that has new knowledge, new emotional tools, and a broader understanding of the facts.

Next, I present a step-by-step process so that you, too, can begin reframing the event you identified using the technique previously taught. This process will help you redefine your memories and free yourself from the emotions that have been shaping your life.

Preparation for Reframing

1. Find a Quiet Place – Choose an environment where you can reflect without interruptions. It could be a quiet room, a garden, or any other place where you feel safe and comfortable.
2. Relax Your Body and Mind – Before beginning the practice, take a few minutes to engage in deep breathing to relax. Slowly inhale through your nose, hold your breath for a few seconds, and exhale through your mouth. Repeat this cycle a few times until your body feels lighter and your mind calmer.
3. Set a Clear Intention – Focus on the idea of redefining the event that triggered your wound of rejection. Your goal should be to understand this event from a new perspective, reducing its emotional burden.

Step into your time machine and return to the moment you identified as the origin of your wound of rejection. Retrace the steps you followed while applying the meditation and reflection technique taught earlier. Visualize the scene, the sounds, the smells, the people involved, and the emotions that arose. The more details you can recall, the better.

Observe your younger self going through the moment. Notice his or her feelings. Recognize the thoughts and emotions that emerge. Identify the automatic thoughts and conclusions you formed about yourself during or after the event. These may include thoughts like: "*I'm not good enough*," "*I don't deserve to be loved*," or "*No one cares about me*." Take note of these thoughts, as they are essential to the reframing process.

Applying Reframing

Recognize current interpretation patterns. Evaluate how you have interpreted the event over the years. Ask yourself: "*How do I describe this experience to myself? What story have I been telling? Do I still believe this interpretation is valid?*"

Consider that your original perception was shaped by pain and a lack of emotional resources at the time. Reflect on how this interpretation has influenced your self-esteem, relationships, and choices. Ask: "*In what ways has this view of the event limited my growth or led me to repetitive patterns?*"

Question limiting beliefs. Examine the beliefs formed based on the event. Ask: "*Does this belief truly correspond to reality? What evidence do I have that this perception is absolute truth?*"

Consider other possibilities. For example, if you believe you were rejected by your father, ask: "*Did this rejec-*

tion really happen, or was he dealing with his own challenges? Could his behavior have had other explanations, such as frustration or a lack of emotional expression skills?" This questioning process helps demystify limiting beliefs and opens space for alternative interpretations, allowing a shift in how you perceive yourself and others.

Reframe the event with a new *'frame.'* To create a new perspective, consider the original context. Remember that you were a child or someone in a developmental phase with limited emotional resources at the time. Ask: "*Now that I see this scene as an observer, what do I notice differently?*" Reflect on the possible motivations and limitations of the other people involved. "*Could my father's behavior have reflected his own inability to deal with emotions or life difficulties? How might he have acted if he had more tools to handle the situation?*"

Reframing the event with this new approach allows you to see the experience in a more understanding and less punitive light.

Transform the experience into a positive learning opportunity. Now, try to identify the growth potential within the event. Ask: "*What has this experience taught me? How can I use it to become stronger?*"

Think about how this situation may have developed qualities in you, such as resilience, courage, or the ability to overcome challenges. Consider whether the event was an opportunity to learn how to set boundaries or develop self-love independent of external validation.

Ask yourself: "*What skills or insights can I extract from this experience to become a better person?*" The goal is to reframe the event so that it is no longer a source of suffering but a catalyst for your personal development.

Integrate the new perspective into your daily life. Finally, reflect on how this new interpretation can influence your actions and thoughts moving forward. Ask yourself: "*How can I apply this new perception in my interactions and daily decisions?*"

Consider that the event, now reinterpreted, can serve as an example of how to handle future challenges more healthily. Think of ways to reinforce this new perspective in your mind, whether through affirmations, journaling, or meaningful conversations.

The goal is for the new frame you have created to become a reference that strengthens your self-esteem and confidence, bringing renewed meaning to what was once only pain.

This reframing process will transform how you see the event and, over time, shape a new way of relating to your emotions and memories, allowing you to live more freely and fully.

By practicing the reframing technique on the event that triggered your feeling of rejection, you have taken another important step in your emotional and behavioral healing journey. Just like the technique used to identify the original event, reframing requires constant repetition until you can apply the acquired knowledge, new facts, and interpretation tools, revisiting the initial event from different perspectives. The goal is to redefine it with a new perspective—one that is true enough to alter the neural structure created when the wound of rejection first emerged.

You will know you have succeeded in this step when you feel as though you have been deceived for a long time. You will realize that countless decisions were made under the influence of this hidden wound. At that moment, you may experience a sense of betrayal, as if you had been misled by your own thoughts and emotions. You will recognize that your life was shaped by this filter of rejection without your conscious awareness. However, after these revelations, you will be overcome by a deep sense of lightness and peace as you realize that you now see yourself as you truly are—someone who is not rejected but rather loved and worthy of love. This feeling is powerful enough to transform the course of your life from this point forward.

But this is only the first stage of the journey. These are the first rays of light that your true self begins to feel after a lifetime of being trapped in the subconscious, afraid to emerge for fear of reliving the pain of rejection. Now that the first rays of light touch your skin, without the oppressive presence of fear, the urge to go further arises. You need to discover what else can be adjusted—what has been shaped by this "*imposter routine*" that has guided your life for so long. What still needs to be acknowledged and transformed? Let's move on to the next steps of this journey.

To better illustrate this, think about computer operating systems like Windows, macOS, or Linux. These systems manage the programs and resources of the device. For example, Windows, launched in 1985, receives constant updates to keep up with technological innovations. Imagine that you have the most modern computer with the latest version of Windows but are using the first version of Microsoft Office, released in 1990. You would have a cutting-edge device but would be limited by outdated software, unable to take full advantage of the system's potential. The system can connect to the cloud and use artificial intelligence, but the old Office version lacks these features. It is obsolete, and this limits the full power of your device.

Similarly, if we compare our brain to a computer, we can say that we have the most advanced hardware known to science, with an operating system of infinite possibilities. However, we are limited by neural synapses formed during poorly interpreted events that remained outdated throughout our lives. Reframing is precisely the process of updating these synapse "*routines*," incorporating new information, tools, and perspectives that have emerged since the formation of the original event. This allows the "*routines*" to function in harmony with our current potential.

After updating the original interpretation of the event, it is essential to trace subsequent moments in your life that reinforced the wound of rejection. Identify significant events that also left emotional impressions and strengthened the already established belief of rejection. These moments need to be reassessed based on the new perspective you have gained so that they can be integrated into your new narrative, now with more appropriate emotional resources.

16

CHILDHOOD

Childhood is a crucial phase for emotional development, as it is during this period that we form our first perceptions of ourselves and the world around us. Significant events during this stage shape beliefs that last a lifetime. To investigate childhood experiences that may have contributed to reinforcing the wound of rejection, consider the following approaches and questions:

- What are my most vivid childhood memories?
- What were the experiences that impacted me the most, both positively and negatively?
- Do I remember moments when I felt excluded, ignored, or unloved?

Create a memory journal. Write down the experiences that come to mind, especially those involving social and family interactions.

Examine how you related to your parents, siblings, and other family members. Ask yourself:

- What was my relationship with my parents like? Was there love and acceptance, or did I feel the need to earn their approval?
- How did my siblings behave towards me? Was there rivalry, jealousy, or exclusion?
- Did I ever feel that I didn't belong in my family or that I wasn't loved?

Create an emotional family tree. Include feelings and interactions that occurred with each family member and highlight those that were significant.

Analyze your childhood friendships and how they affected your sense of belonging. Ask:

- Did I have close friends, or did I often feel lonely?
- Were there moments when I was excluded from games or groups? How did I feel at the time?
- Did I experience bullying or criticism from peers? What were the words or actions that hurt me the most?

Create a list of significant friendships. For each friendship, write down positive and negative moments you remember, highlighting any experiences of rejection.

School is an environment where many wounds of rejection can arise. Ask:

- What were my school experiences like? Was there a group of classmates who accepted me, or did I feel out of place?

- Do I remember any situations where I was ridiculed or ignored by teachers or classmates?
- What were my difficulties in socializing or expressing myself at school?

Create a mind map of your school life. Include events, friendships, teachers, and significant moments. Analyze how these experiences shaped your perception of yourself.

After reviewing your memories and identifying the events that contributed to reinforcing the existing wound of rejection, repeat the reframing process for these events. Now, view them from an updated perspective, considering that the original event has already been reframed. It is important to repeat the process with these later events because, just as they reinforced the original wound of rejection, by reframing them, you will strengthen the new perspective you are building. With each reframed event throughout your life, this new vision will become stronger and more powerful, replacing the old, outdated version of your neural pathways.

Adolescence

Adolescence is a phase of intense physical, emotional, and social transformations. During this stage, the desire for social acceptance and the search for one's own identity become stronger. It is a period where feelings of inadequacy, rejection, and exclusion can be particularly painful and impactful, as the adolescent brain is more sensitive to these experiences. Events that occur during this phase can potentially reinforce the feelings of rejection formed in childhood.

Ask yourself if there were situations where you felt excluded, ridiculed, or inadequate in relation to your peers. These experiences may have occurred at school, in sports activities, among friends, or in other social contexts. Reflect on how these episodes may have reinforced the already existing feeling of rejection.

- Were there moments when I was excluded from social activities or events?
- Was I ever a target of bullying or derogatory comments? How did that affect how I see myself?
- Were there situations where I felt I did not meet the expectations of my friends or peers?

During adolescence, relationships with parents and other family members can become turbulent, especially due to the desire for greater autonomy. Reevaluate whether there were moments when you felt you did not receive the support, attention, or affection you expected from your family. These experiences may have reinforced the belief that you were not valued or loved.

- Did I feel that my opinions or feelings were not considered by my parents?
- Were there times when I felt negatively compared to my siblings or relatives?

- Were there occasions when I was punished or criticized in a way that made me feel inadequate or rejected?

First romantic relationships or romantic interests can be a source of emotional vulnerability. Rejections, breakups, or heartbreaks may have left deep marks and reinforced the feeling of not being worthy of affection or love. Reflect on these experiences and how they influenced the way you perceived yourself.

- Was I ever rejected by someone I was interested in? How did that experience affect me?
- Were there relationships in which I felt insecure or constantly afraid of being abandoned?
- Did these experiences change the way I relate to others?

The pressure to perform well in school may have been a source of stress and, in some cases, may have reinforced feelings of inadequacy. If there were failures, constant criticism, or comparisons with other students, this may have strengthened the idea that you were not capable or valuable.

- Was I criticized for not meeting certain grades or academic expectations?
- Did I feel that I was constantly compared to other students, siblings, or peers in terms of academic performance?

- How did I deal with academic failures or difficulties during this phase?

Adolescence is marked by bodily changes and the construction of self-image. Issues related to physical appearance, acne, weight, or other concerns may have generated insecurities and fueled the feeling of not being accepted.

- Did I feel insecure or uncomfortable with my body during adolescence?
- How did other people's opinions about my physical appearance affect my self-esteem?
- Did I try to conform to beauty standards or behaviors to be accepted?

By identifying relevant events from this phase, use reframing to reinterpret these experiences with a new perspective, now considering the emotional resources and maturity you have today. This will allow you to redefine these moments and strengthen your new perception, reprogramming the "*automatic routines*" of defense mechanisms and creating a healthier and more positive vision of yourself.

Early Adulthood

Early adulthood is marked by new responsibilities and challenges, such as starting a career, seeking financial independence, and forming more serious relationships.

Social expectations increase, and there is greater pressure to "*succeed*" in life. During this phase, negative events can intensify the hidden wound of rejection. As you explore this stage, it is important to identify situations that reinforced the feeling of rejection and how these experiences may have influenced your choices and behaviors.

Starting a professional life often involves difficulties, receiving criticism, and dealing with failures. Negative work experiences, such as layoffs, rejection in job applications, or lack of recognition, may have reinforced the feeling of not being good enough. Reflect on these moments to understand how they have affected your self-esteem and self-perception.

- Have I been rejected in job interviews or promotions? How did these experiences impact my confidence?
- Have I ever felt that my work was not valued or that I did not receive the recognition I deserved?
- Have I ever felt incapable of meeting the expectations of bosses or colleagues?

Challenges related to financial independence, such as dealing with debt, bills, or difficulties in sustaining oneself, can amplify feelings of failure or rejection.

- Have I felt overwhelmed by financial or professional responsibilities?
- Have I struggled to reach financial goals I set for myself?

- Have I been disappointed for not being able to provide more comfort or financial support for myself or my loved ones?

Romantic relationships tend to become deeper and more significant. Painful breakups, betrayals, or feelings of rejection in serious relationships can be particularly impactful and reinforce emotional rejection patterns.

- Have I been abandoned or betrayed by a partner? How did this affect how I see myself and trust others?
- Do I feel incapable of establishing healthy relationships due to past experiences?
- Have there been moments when I felt inadequate or unloved in a relationship?

Maintaining friendships and feeling part of a group can be challenging in early adulthood, especially when dealing with changes like moving to a new city or starting a new job. Feeling excluded from social events, struggling to maintain friendships, or not feeling a sense of belonging can fuel the feeling of rejection.

- Have I felt excluded from activities or social circles?
- Do I struggle to maintain friendships due to fear of rejection or abandonment?
- Do I feel like I put too much effort into pleasing others in order to gain acceptance?

Comparing oneself to peers in terms of career, financial success, or personal achievements is natural.

However, when these comparisons lead to feelings of inferiority or inadequacy, they can reinforce the perception of rejection or failure.

- Do I often compare myself to friends or acquaintances who seem more successful? How does this affect my self-esteem?
- Do I feel pressured to achieve certain milestones, such as getting married, buying a house, or advancing in my career?
- Are the expectations I set for myself realistic, or am I trying to meet external standards?

It is common to feel regret over past choices or paths not taken. These feelings can contribute to a negative self-perception, reinforcing the belief that wrong decisions were the result of an inherent inability or inadequacy.

- Do I regret choices I made in my personal or professional life? How does this affect how I see myself?
- Do I fear making new decisions because of past failures?
- How do I deal with the feeling that I could have done better or taken a different path?

The pressure to achieve a certain physical appearance or meet an ideal health standard can deeply impact self-esteem. Issues with weight, health, or physical appearance can contribute to feelings of rejection or inadequacy.

- Does my self-image make me feel insecure? Do I often compare myself to others?
- Do I struggle to maintain healthy habits? How does this affect my self-esteem?
- Have I ever felt the need to improve my appearance in order to be accepted or valued?

Now, use this framework to reinterpret your experiences with an updated perspective. Consider the abilities and knowledge you have gained over time to redefine these events, strengthening your new outlook. This will allow you to build a more positive and empowered narrative, overcoming the hidden wound of rejection.

Romantic Relationships

Romantic relationships are one of the most significant areas to explore when it comes to wounds of rejection, as they deal directly with issues of acceptance, affection, and intimacy. Traumatic or painful events in past relationships may have left deep marks that reinforced wounds of rejection, influencing how you approach current and future relationships.

A breakup can be a painful experience, especially if it happened abruptly, unexpectedly, or traumatically. The feeling of not being wanted or being abandoned can fuel the perception of being unworthy of love. Analyzing the breakup and its surrounding context can help redefine what happened.

- Was I left abruptly, or did I feel that the breakup was unfair? How did that affect my self-perception?
- Do I blame myself for past breakups? Do I feel like I could have done something differently to prevent them?
- Am I afraid to get involved again because of a traumatic breakup experience?

Betrayal can be devastating, as it directly impacts trust and self-image. The feeling of being replaced or deceived can create deep insecurity and reinforce the wound of rejection. It is important to analyze the circumstances, understand the factors involved, and work on rebuilding trust in yourself and others.

- Have I been betrayed by a partner? How did that experience affect my trust in relationships?
- Do I feel that the betrayal was somehow proof of my inadequacy or lack of worth?
- Do I frequently distrust new partners out of fear of being betrayed again?

The pain of being rejected by someone you love or admire can be a significant experience. This type of rejection can occur when trying to initiate a relationship or even within a relationship, where feelings are not reciprocated with the same intensity.

- Have I been rejected by someone I genuinely wanted to be with? How did that affect my self-esteem?

- Have I felt ignored or unreciprocated in a relationship? How did I deal with that situation?
- Do I try to protect myself from rejection by avoiding expressing my feelings or initiating new relationships?

Relationships where there is a power imbalance or manipulation can leave a person feeling powerless or dependent on the other for validation. This can reinforce the idea that love and affection are conditional and must constantly be "*earned*."

- Have I been in a relationship where my partner tried to control my feelings or behaviors?
- Did I feel that I constantly had to make an effort to be accepted or loved within the relationship?
- Did I tolerate mistreatment or disrespect out of fear of losing the relationship?

If you had difficulty communicating your needs, desires, or setting boundaries in a relationship, you might have felt invisible or undervalued. A lack of assertive communication can result in accumulated frustration and resentment, reinforcing the feeling of rejection.

- Did I feel guilty for expressing what I truly wanted or needed in a relationship?
- Was I afraid to set boundaries, fearing that my partner would pull away or stop liking me?
- Were my needs often ignored or diminished by my partner?

The tendency to idealize a partner or expect them to fill all emotional voids can lead to constant frustration. When the partner does not meet these expectations, you may feel rejected or unloved.

- Did I put my partner on a pedestal, expecting my emotional problems to be solved?
- Did I feel devalued when my partner did not meet my expectations, even if they were unrealistic?
- Did I try to change my partner to fit the ideal image I had in mind?

When exploring these areas in romantic relationships, it is essential to apply reframing to reinterpret experiences from an updated and mature perspective. This means analyzing past events, recognizing how you have changed and grown since then, and updating your "*routines*." By doing so, you can overcome feelings of rejection and build a healthier, more balanced approach to future relationships.

Marital Relationships

In marital relationships, long-term commitment and daily coexistence bring forth a different dynamic compared to other romantic relationships. Issues such as communication, division of responsibilities, intimacy, expectations, and changes over time can deeply affect how partners feel accepted or rejected. The hidden wound of rejection in a marriage can gradually intensify and be fueled by everyday behaviors, attitudes, and interactions.

When a spouse constantly criticizes or fails to support their partner's choices and achievements, it can create a sense of devaluation and rejection. These criticisms can be direct or manifest as a lack of recognition or praise.

- Does my partner frequently criticize my decisions or actions? How does that make me feel about my self-worth?
- Do I feel that no matter how hard I try, I am never good enough to please my spouse?
- Have I ever given up on pursuing my dreams or ambitions because I felt that my partner did not believe in me?

An imbalance in household chores, financial responsibilities, or childcare duties can lead to resentment. Feeling overburdened while the partner does not contribute equally can reinforce a sense of being undervalued or taken for granted.

- Do I take on most of the responsibilities at home or in raising our children? Do I feel that this division is fair?
- Have I ever felt invisible or overwhelmed, as if my contributions were seen as an obligation rather than an effort?
- Do I try to compensate for my spouse's lack of participation by putting in extra effort, hoping it will improve our relationship?

A decrease in physical or emotional intimacy in marriage can be a significant source of rejection. When a partner seems distant or avoids moments of closeness, it can be interpreted as a lack of desire or interest, directly impacting self-esteem and the feeling of acceptance.

- Does my partner avoid or seem disinterested in moments of physical intimacy? How does that affect me emotionally?
- Do I feel that our emotional bond has weakened over time? Does that make me feel less valued?
- Am I afraid to address intimacy issues with my spouse, fearing rejection or criticism?

When spouses do not share the same goals or when their priorities change over time, it can create a sense of distance and rejection. A lack of alignment in life objectives can lead to feelings of disconnection and dissatisfaction.

- Do I feel that my spouse and I are heading in different directions when it comes to our life goals?
- Have I ever felt pressured to give up on my dreams to meet my spouse's expectations or priorities?
- Is there a lack of mutual support for our ambitions? How does that affect our relationship and my self-esteem?

If the same conflicts arise repeatedly without resolution, a couple may become trapped in a cycle of frustration and resentment. Negative communication patterns—

such as prolonged silence, harsh criticism, or constant arguments—reinforce the feeling of rejection and can impact the perception of acceptance in the relationship.

- Do the same problems seem to come up constantly in our relationship? Are we able to resolve them constructively?
- How do I feel after an argument? Do I feel heard, or do I feel like my concerns are dismissed?
- Do I avoid arguments out of fear of how they might end, even if it means suppressing my feelings?

As spouses age or go through different life stages—such as parenthood, retirement, or career changes—expectations and needs can shift. If these changes are not discussed or acknowledged, feelings of dissatisfaction and rejection may arise.

- Have the changes in our lives created distance between us? How have these transitions affected our emotional connection?
- Did I expect my spouse to change or behave in a certain way, but that did not happen? How did I cope with those unmet expectations?
- Have my partner's priorities changed over time? Do I feel like I have been pushed to the background?

In a marriage, emotional neglect occurs when one partner's emotional needs are consistently unmet. This can lead to a persistent sense of loneliness and rejection, even within the relationship.

- Do I feel that my emotional needs are often ignored or minimized by my spouse?
- How long have I felt lonely in the relationship? What changed to make this happen?
- Do I seek validation or comfort outside the relationship? What does that say about my current emotional needs?

By revisiting the events in a marital relationship that have contributed to wounds of rejection, the goal is to reframe these experiences, bringing a new understanding of the challenges and changes that have occurred over time. Repeating the process of redefining these experiences will help strengthen a new perspective, allowing the spouse to see the relationship with greater clarity and compassion. This paves the way for healthier dialogue, deeper emotional connection, and, potentially, a renewed mutual commitment to growth and happiness.

Relationship with Your Children

When a parent carries a hidden wound of rejection, this feeling deeply influences the way they relate to their children. Insecurities, fears, and negative beliefs associated with this wound tend to be unconsciously projected onto parental relationships, affecting family dynamics and causing children to develop feelings of rejection or inadequacy. That's why it is crucial for parents to reflect on how these unresolved issues shape their attitudes, behaviors, and expectations toward their children. This awareness is essential, as these influences can directly impact the emotional development of children, leaving marks that may last a lifetime.

Parents who feel rejected may try to fulfill their emotional needs through their children's success, setting high expectations or projecting their fears onto them. When children fail to meet these expectations, parents may unintentionally express disappointment or frustration, which children can perceive as rejection.

- Do I expect my children to achieve certain goals or behave in a way that validates my self-worth? How might this be affecting my relationship with them?
- Do I feel frustrated when my children don't meet my expectations? How do I express this frustration to them?
- Are my personal insecurities leading me to pressure my children to be "*better*" or "*more successful*" than I was?

Some parents become overly controlling or overprotective, trying to ensure that their children do not suffer or make mistakes. Although this intention may seem positive, it can prevent children from developing autonomy, resilience, and self-confidence.

- Am I afraid to allow my children to make mistakes? Why does this affect me so much?
- Is my need to control or protect inhibiting my children's freedom and development? How might this be impacting their self-perception?

- Do I constantly intervene in my children's lives to prevent them from experiencing pain, failure, or rejection? What might this be teaching them about dealing with challenges?

Parents struggling with wounds of rejection may unconsciously seek validation and approval from their children to feel accepted. This dynamic can create a role reversal, where children feel pressured to meet their parents' emotional needs rather than receiving the support they require.

- Do I depend on my children's approval to feel like a good parent? How might this search for validation be affecting our relationship?
- Have I noticed that I feel hurt or upset when my children don't respond the way I expected? Why does this happen?
- Do I feel rejected when my children prefer to spend time with others or engage in activities without my participation? How do I handle this situation?

When children don't behave as expected or display challenging behaviors, parents with a hidden wound of rejection may react disproportionately, perceiving these actions as a personal attack or direct rejection. This can result in excessive punishments, emotional withdrawal, or manipulative tactics to force obedience.

- Do I interpret my children's rebellious or disobedient behavior as a rejection of me? Why?

- Are my reactions overly intense in conflict situations with my children? How does this affect our relationship and their well-being?
- Do I try to impose authority or control out of fear of losing my children's respect or love?

For some parents, the wound of rejection makes it difficult to express genuine affection. They may fear that their affection will be rejected or that showing vulnerability will expose them, leading to a colder or more distant relationship. As a result, children may interpret this lack of affection as rejection.

- Do I find it difficult to express affection spontaneously to my children? What fears might be behind this?
- Have I ever avoided affectionate moments with my children for fear that they wouldn't reciprocate or appreciate the gesture?
- Do I avoid deep emotional connections with my children out of fear of getting hurt? What can I do to change this?

When parents feel insecure or rejected, they may unconsciously compare their children to others as a way to encourage improvement or justify their own feelings. This can cause children to feel inadequate and insecure, undermining their self-esteem.

- Do I compare my children to others, thinking it might motivate them to improve? How might this be affecting their confidence?

- Do I use comparison as a way to cope with my own frustrations or fears regarding my children's behavior?
- Am I projecting my own insecurities and expectations when comparing my children to others?

Recognizing how the hidden wound of rejection influences the way you interact with your children is a crucial step in breaking the cycle and fostering a healthier, more loving environment. By adjusting your behaviors and redefining your attitudes toward them, you can create a space where your children feel accepted, supported, and loved. This process of redefinition and healing also benefits the entire family dynamic, allowing your children to grow with stronger self-esteem and the emotional security needed to face life's challenges.

Now that you have reviewed your life, identifying events that reinforced your original wound of rejection and practiced reframing each of them, your new perspective on life is stronger and more powerful. You are likely already feeling the effects of this transformation: you have become a different person—more aware and conscious of the control you have over your emotions. The people around you, especially those closest to you, have already noticed these changes, and you are beginning to enjoy the benefits of this new mindset, with new feelings and behaviors. Life has become lighter and more fluid; the energy that was once spent maintaining defense mechanisms is now being directed toward more productive actions. You feel more motivated, more energetic, and an increasing sense of capability and empowerment is replacing the fear that once dominated.

However, there is still work to be done. Years of being guided by the hidden wound of rejection have led your brain, as the excellent resource manager it is, to create "*routines*" of automatic responses that operate unconsciously, keeping your life on "*autopilot.*" Now, you are ready to begin identifying the stimuli or triggers that activate these automatic patterns and take conscious control over them. It is time to step out of autopilot mode and switch to manual control, intentionally managing your reactions and directing your life according to your conscious choices.

17

AUTOMATIC REACTIONS

After becoming aware that my life was running on autopilot, I realized I had drifted far from my dreams and desires. I embarked on a journey of self-discovery, identified the hidden wound of rejection that had controlled my life for so many years, and traced it back to its origin. I brought the initial event to light and repeated the process with as many subsequent events as I could remember, using the techniques presented in the previous chapters. However, there was still one more step to overcome in this journey: identifying the stimuli and triggers that activated my automatic reactions—powerful mechanisms created by my brain to protect me from the pain of rejection.

I felt lighter than ever before, as if I were finally in control, steering my own ship. After all, I had rewritten the story of my life, understood countless events that had trapped me, and now saw the world from a new perspective. It was a sunny Sunday with pleasant weather in the city where I live. My wife and I decided to have lunch at a nice restaurant—something we hadn't done in a long time. The restaurant was right by the sea, overlooking a paradise-like coastline. Since parking nearby was difficult, I left the car about 700 meters away in a plaza, which gave us the opportunity to walk along the shore, admire the scenery, and observe the movement of tourists. It was an enjoyable walk, as it always is.

During our walk, my wife commented, "*See, my love? This is what I always say. Why don't we do this more often? We live here; we don't need a special occasion to enjoy this view—we just have to come.*" I agreed with her and said we should do this more often. However, I felt a slight emotional discomfort.

We arrived at the restaurant and had a wonderful meal. The food was delicious, and we were happy and excited. We had two bottles of wine, and the moment felt magical. By the time we left the restaurant, it was late, and the view was even more breathtaking. On our way back, my wife brought up the topic again: "*In the past, we lived near here and used to take morning walks along this shore. I would love to live here again, but it seems like the more I wish for it, the further away we get.*" At that moment, I felt a wave of heat rush through my body, and I snapped: "*Seriously? After such a special day, you want to end it like this? Complaining? Instead of enjoying the moment and this view?*"

And just like that, our perfect day was over.

We went home upset with each other. A little later, an inner voice questioned me: "*What was that, Gerson? You've been studying emotional management so much... How could you fall into this trap? Look at how you reacted. Did you even pay attention to what your wife was saying? You don't even remember her exact words, and yet you exploded! Haven't you overcome this? Does this reaction belong to your current version of yourself?*" At that moment, I fell silent and remained quiet for the rest of the day, partly because I was still under the effects of the wine.

The next morning, when I woke up, I started reflecting on what had happened. This wasn't the first time something like this had occurred; in fact, these situations had become common in our lives over the past few years. However, I had never stopped to reflect on what was really happening—I simply believed that my wife had ruined the moment. But something had changed within me: I had implemented updates in my neural pathways and was seeing life from a new perspective. Since I was now accustomed to revisiting events where I felt rejected, that morning, almost automatically, I started analyzing the situation and using my new mindset to understand what had happened.

That's when I realized that I reacted automatically to certain stimuli that my protective mechanisms identified as signs of potential rejection. My wife often used expressions like "*I wish*" or "*I would love to,*" and those words, which might mean nothing special to someone else, were like lighting a powder keg for me—someone who carried the deep-seated belief of not being enough. As her life partner, whenever she said, "*I wish,*" I interpreted it as her desiring something I was unable to provide, support, or facilitate. As a result, I always perceived these statements as criticisms or complaints, when in reality, she was sharing a dream, a goal, or an invitation for me to be part of her desires.

By seeing the situation from this new perspective, I was able to identify the trigger for my automatic reactions. Unlike the countless times in the past when I would withdraw in silence, waiting for her to start a conversation as if nothing had happened, this time, I felt deeply uncomfortable with what had occurred. My love for her was no longer suffocated by the fear of rejection, and my fear of not being accepted was no longer strong enough to stop me from initiating a dialogue, expressing my feelings, and apologizing—not just for what had happened that day, but for all the previous instances.

For the first time in decades of marriage, I explained to her how phrases like "*I wish*" or "*I would love to*" triggered an automatic protective response in me, leading to an emotional outburst. And I told her that now that I was aware of this trigger, I would no longer react automatically or unconsciously.

At that moment, I felt that another step was being completed, and my liberation from the chains of hidden rejection was becoming more real.

Now, it's your turn. Stop, reflect, and identify the triggers that activate your automatic reactions—those that harm different areas of your life. The reflection exercise below will help you with this step.

This step may be more challenging and take more time because, until now, everything we have done has been theoretical or about planning. Now, we are ready to go to the "*battlefront.*" This is the moment to put our new life perspective to the test—to expose ourselves to the world. After identifying and redefining as many of our protective mechanisms as possible, it is time to test our new "*routines*" and take control of our lives in critical moments—moments that, in the past, we left in the hands of our wounded, childlike version with limited resources. Now is the time to live our upgrade.

This exercise will help you better understand your automatic reactions by bringing awareness to the emotional triggers that affect your life. Follow the steps calmly and sincerely, allowing yourself to explore memories and feelings. This exercise is designed to help you identify and transform these triggers so that you can respond to situations with clarity and self-control, rather than being led by autopilot.

Reliving a Recent Event

- Remember a recent situation where you reacted intensely and automatically—perhaps with irritation, sadness, blockage, or another difficult emotion. Choose something that had an impact, even if it seemed small to others.
- Write down the event in detail: where you were, who was with you, what was said, and how you felt at that moment. Don't hold back on descriptions; the more detailed, the better.
- Identify the reaction: What was the first thing you felt and did? How intense was your response? Write about it honestly.

Discovering the Trigger

- Observe the words or actions of the other person that triggered your reaction. Try to isolate the exact moment when your mood or feelings changed.
- Ask yourself: What were the specific words or actions that affected me the most? Was there a phrase, expression, or tone that triggered my reaction?
- Feel what's behind the trigger: Close your eyes and reflect on what those words or actions mean to you. Ask yourself:
  - Do these words or actions touch on an insecurity of mine?
  - What exactly did I feel at the time? Was it fear, sadness, anger, frustration?
  - Do these feelings connect to a specific memory from my life?

Connecting with the Origin of the Feeling

- Go back in time and find the first moment you remember feeling something similar. It could be a memory from childhood, adolescence, or even adulthood. Let the memories come without judging or censoring them.
- Recall the scene: Where were you? Who was with you? What happened? How did you feel?
- Ask yourself: What thoughts and emotions does this memory bring up today? Is it possible that you

still carry some of these beliefs or feelings with you, influencing your reactions in the present?

- Write down this memory and describe how it connects to the recent event you chose. How do these experiences relate? Does this trigger seem to be activated by a specific fear, insecurity, or feeling of rejection?

Reframing the Trigger

- Look at the recent event from a new perspective: Now that you have identified a possible origin, ask yourself how you could have reacted differently if you hadn't been overtaken by emotion. Write an ideal version of what could have happened.
- Reinterpret the meaning of the other person's words or actions: Try to see what was said or done in a neutral way. Remember that what the other person said was not necessarily related to your personal worth but often reflects that person's own feelings and desires.
- Replace the old belief with a new one: If, for example, the old belief was "*I'm not good enough,*" transform it into "*I am enough just as I am, and I am evolving.*" Write down this new belief to reaffirm it to yourself.

Committing to New Reactions

- Create a list of conscious responses: Imagine that similar situations will happen in the future. How would you like to respond? Make a list of actions and reactions you'd like to incorporate, such as taking a deep breath, asking more about the other person's perspective, or expressing your feelings more calmly.

- Practice self-observation: Make a commitment that every time you notice the trigger approaching, you will remember the new interpretation and the responses you want to program. Write down any progress or lessons in your journal.

Maintenance and Reinforcement Exercise

- Reflect on similar situations throughout the week: At the end of each day, take note of any triggers that appeared and how you reacted. Celebrate every small progress, and use any setbacks as opportunities to understand yourself better.
- Apply supportive self-talk: If you notice an intense reaction about to surface, calm yourself with reassuring words like, "*I am in control of my emotions,*" or "*I can listen and understand without reacting automatically.*"
- Revisit the exercise regularly: From time to time, go through this exercise again to analyze new situations, update your beliefs, and strengthen your ability to respond consciously.

The same approach can be applied to avoidance behaviors that stem from hidden wounds of rejection. By bringing to awareness the connections between everyday situations and the habits you use to escape difficult emotions, you can begin transforming these triggers and developing healthier responses aligned with your well-being. Follow the steps with patience, honesty, and openness to reflection.

Reliving a Recent Escape Event

- Recall a recent situation where you resorted to an avoidance behavior, such as compulsive eating, smoking, getting lost in social media, or making unnecessary purchases. Choose a moment that had an emotional impact.
- Describe the situation in detail: where you were, what you were doing before, how the avoidance behavior started, and how you felt. Be specific and include details such as thoughts or emotions that preceded the action.
- Write down how you felt immediately after the behavior: Did you feel relief, guilt, emptiness, or something else? Be honest in your description.

Identifying the Trigger

- Reflect on the moment when you felt the urge to engage in the avoidance behavior. What was the starting point? Was there a specific situation, an interaction with someone, or an internal thought?
- Try to identify the words, actions, or feelings that may have triggered your reaction. Ask yourself:
    - What exactly happened before I acted this way?

    - Was there any thought or feeling of inadequacy, rejection, or frustration?
- Close your eyes and feel what lies behind the trigger. Ask yourself:
    - Does this touch on any insecurity or old emotional wound?
    - What emotion arose at that moment? Fear, sadness, anger, anxiety?
    - Is this emotion connected to any past experience?

Connecting with the Origin of the Feeling

- Search your memory for the first moment you remember feeling something similar. It could be a memory from childhood, adolescence, or even adulthood. Let the images surface without judgment.
- Recall the scene calmly: where you were, who was with you, what happened? How did you feel at that moment?
- Ask yourself:
    - Does this memory still influence my feelings and reactions today?
    - What beliefs about myself or the world were formed at that moment?
    - Do these beliefs justify or reinforce my current avoidance behavior?
- Write about the connection between this memory and the recent event. Reflect on how the past experience may be reinforcing your need to escape from emotions.

Reframing the Trigger

- Review the recent event from a new perspective: now that you have identified the origin, ask yourself how you could have acted differently if you were not caught in the impulse to escape the emotion. Write down this ideal version.
- Reinterpret the meaning of the trigger: does what happened really require an avoidance behavior? Often, it is a disproportionate response. Replace this interpretation with something more neutral and realistic.
- Replace the old limiting belief with an empowering one. For example:
    - From: "*I can't handle rejection.*"
    - To: "*I am capable of managing my emotions and can choose responses that benefit me.*"
    - Write down this new belief and repeat it whenever you feel the urge to resort to avoidance behaviors.

Committing to New Reactions

- Create a list of healthy alternatives: for each avoidance behavior, list at least one alternative action. For example:
    - Instead of compulsive eating, practice breathing exercises or meditation.
    - Instead of excessive social media use, read a book or go for a walk.
    - Instead of overworking, schedule breaks to relax and take care of yourself.

- Visualize future situations: imagine similar situations happening again. How would you like to react? Make a list of conscious actions to apply in these situations.
- Practice recognizing escape signals: whenever you notice a trigger, follow the alternatives you noted and apply one of them in the moment.

Maintenance and Reinforcement Exercise

- Reflect daily: at the end of each day, write down if any triggers appeared and how you reacted. Celebrate each small step forward and treat any setbacks as learning opportunities.
- Practice internal dialogue: develop supportive phrases for challenging moments, such as:
  - I am in control of my choices.
  - I can face this emotion without running away.
- Revisit the exercise periodically: use it to explore new triggers, update your beliefs, and strengthen your healthy responses.

Reprogramming your automatic reactions is the final stage of the healing journey. At this stage, you consciously take control of your life, removing it from autopilot. This was only possible because you were able to identify the origin of your hidden wound of rejection, work on reframing your perspective, and map all the subsequent events that previously reinforced this wound. By reframing them, they now strengthen your new perspective.

With this new understanding of events, the hidden wound of rejection no longer holds power over you. You now realize that you were not actually rejected—you simply interpreted it that way because you lacked the tools and knowledge you have today. Now that you feel differently, you can take the "*routine*" that your brain created to activate defense mechanisms, reprogram it, and shift from automatic mode to manual mode.

From now on, whenever you encounter the triggers that previously activated your avoidance mechanisms, you will consciously and fully control how to handle the situation. This will allow you to start making choices and decisions in a completely conscious way—because now, you are in control of your life.

18

THE JOURNEY SO FAR

So far, we have seen that all of us, to varying degrees, have been shaped by automatic reactions: "*routines*" created by our child brain to cope with events similar to those that gave rise to the hidden wound of rejection within us.

We have learned to identify, in our behaviors and emotions, the traits that indicate which defense mechanisms are most present in our lives. With this information, we used relaxation and reflection techniques to guide our minds on a journey through time, witnessing the exact moment when our younger selves experienced the traumatic event that gave rise to the hidden wound of rejection.

By identifying it, we learned the technique of reframing, which allowed us to alter the way we viewed that event, providing a new understanding of the facts. As a result, we freed ourselves from the hidden wound of rejection that had imprisoned us for so long. We also applied reframing to as many subsequent events as we could remember, reinforcing our new narrative and updating our feelings in accordance with the knowledge and cognitive tools we currently possess. In other words, we stopped feeling like children and started acting like adults.

Finally, we learned to identify the stimuli or triggers that activated our neural programming, leading us to react automatically whenever we perceived any hint of possible rejection. With the technique of identifying and reprogramming this "*routine*," we managed to update the "*routines*" that once operated on autopilot. These routines had prevented us from hearing, seeing, thinking, and understanding before reacting or escaping. Now, we act with awareness: we have stepped out of autopilot and taken control of our actions.

All stages of the transformation process have been covered. You now know every step necessary to reprogram your mind and update the "*routines*" that have guided your life. However, just like with any learning, practice is required. Think of how you install a program on your computer or phone: the same happens with your brain. Each learning experience is like a new program or app. The difference is that, to install a new "*routine*" or brain synapse, repetition and habit are needed.

Think of something you have learned, whether it's a new language, playing an instrument, driving, or any everyday task. The initial learning may have taken only a few hours, but it was only through repeated practice, over numerous attempts, that this skill became automatic. This happened because you managed to "*install*" this new skill in your brain.

This is exactly what you need to do now with what you have learned in this book. By consciously and persistently practicing the techniques discussed, reflecting on your behaviors, identifying the signs of the hidden wound of rejection and its origin, applying the reframing exercises, and recognizing the stimuli that lead you to react automatically, you will understand these stimuli, update your perspectives, and start acting consciously and in control.

Over time, all of these steps and processes will transform into your new "*routines*," which will operate automatically – but this time, in your favor. In this way, you will lead your life consciously, heading in the direction you desire.

Empathy

Through the practice of the exercises proposed so far, you have begun a transformative process in a natural and progressive way: you have developed empathy and, as a result, started to reduce your level of egocentrism. This is a significant milestone in your journey toward freeing yourself from The Hidden Wound of Rejection, as it marks the transition from a self-centered perspective to a broader, more connected view of the world around you.

When under the influence of The Hidden Wound of Rejection, we believe that all external actions, words, or situations are directly related to us. This perception places us in a state of emotional hypervigilance, where we are constantly alert, meticulously analyzing behaviors, gestures, and words. We either seek approval incessantly or protect ourselves from potential rejection, creating an emotionally exhausting cycle.

This way of living traps us in involuntary egocentrism, where we focus excessively on our own needs, pains, and fears—often without considering the perspectives and emotions of others. It is important to emphasize that this egocentrism is not the result of intentional selfishness but rather an unconscious defense mechanism triggered by the fear of rejection.

However, by practicing self-awareness and applying the exercises suggested in this book, you have begun to break this cycle. You have learned to observe your emotions and reactions more clearly, to question limiting beliefs, and to reinterpret the intentions of others. This process has unlocked your empathy, allowing you to see that not all external actions are about you. As a result, you have gained a deeper understanding of others' thoughts, feelings, and intentions—even when they are disconnected from your own experiences.

The Importance of Continuing to Cultivate Empathy

Developing empathy is not a destination but an ongoing journey. To maintain this new version of yourself—free from the dominance of The Hidden Wound of Rejection—it is essential to continue cultivating empathy as a daily practice. Here are some reasons why this is so important:

Strengthens Emotional Resilience

Empathy helps you understand that adversity and rejection are part of life but do not define who you are. This strengthens your ability to face challenges without falling into a constant state of alert.

Promotes More Authentic Connections

Relationships built on empathy are deeper and more genuine. By truly connecting with others, you build bonds that sustain your self-esteem and reduce feelings of emotional isolation.

Reduces Excessive Personalization

When you understand that other people's actions do not revolve around you, your mind gains space to interpret events more neutrally, easing the emotional burden of external situations.

Prevents the Return of Old Patterns

The Hidden Wound of Rejection may try to resurface in moments of vulnerability. The continuous practice of empathy acts as an "*emotional muscle,*" strengthening your ability to avoid relapses.

Keep Developing Your Empathy

Practice Active Listening

When listening to others, genuinely seek to understand what they are feeling, without interrupting or judging.

Cultivate Compassion

Develop the ability to put yourself in someone else's shoes, even when their actions or words seem difficult to understand.

Regularly Reflect on Your Reactions

Ask yourself: "Am I interpreting this situation based on what actually happened or on my past insecurities?"

Celebrate Small Wins

Acknowledge each moment when you responded with empathy rather than egocentrism. Small victories create significant change.

Keep a Reflection Journal

Write about your experiences, noting how practicing empathy has influenced your interactions and emotions over time.

The practice of empathy is a fundamental pillar in your ongoing transformation. It not only reduces egocentrism but also creates a healthier emotional space where The Hidden Wound of Rejection loses its power over you. By continuing to develop and apply empathy, you strengthen yourself emotionally, connect more deeply with the world, and keep alive this renewed version of yourself—freer, more balanced, and more self-aware.

Compassion

As empathy is applied, it transforms the way you relate to your emotions and the world around you. This natural growth of empathy also awakens another powerful element of healing: compassion. Compassion goes beyond understanding the emotions of others; it is the ability to deeply feel, to wish to alleviate suffering, and to take action—whether toward yourself or others.

Throughout your journey of freeing yourself from The Hidden Wound of Rejection, compassion plays an essential role. Both self-compassion and compassion for others help dissolve accumulated pain, create new emotional perspectives, and sustain the necessary change for your new life direction.

Self-Compassion

Self-compassion is fundamental to breaking the patterns of self-criticism and shame often associated with The Hidden Wound of Rejection. When shaped by this feeling, we tend to be harsh on ourselves, believing we are inadequate or to blame for our circumstances. However, practicing self-compassion offers a powerful alternative:

- Acceptance of Wounds: Allowing yourself to acknowledge pain without judgment is liberating. Self-compassion creates a safe space to validate your emotions and understand that they are part of the human experience.
- Reduction of Self-Criticism: Instead of punishing yourself for not meeting unrealistic expectations, you begin to treat yourself with the same kindness you would offer to a dear friend.
- Building Resilience: Practicing self-compassion helps you face challenges with greater emotional balance, reducing the impact of painful memories and strengthening your ability to move forward.

Self-compassion is the foundation of internal healing. Without it, it is difficult to create an emotional environment conducive to freeing yourself from the past and embracing a new version of yourself.

Compassion for Others

The Hidden Wound of Rejection traps us in our own pain, making it difficult to see the emotions and needs of others. However, as compassion for others grows, a powerful transformation takes place:

- Understanding Others with Empathy: Compassion for others helps us recognize that the people around us also face challenges, fears, and limitations. This awareness pulls us out of emotional isolation and connects us to the universal aspect of human experience.
- Reducing Resentment: Seeing the limitations and motivations of those who have hurt us alleviates the weight of resentment. This does not mean justifying negative actions, but rather freeing yourself from emotions that imprison you.
- Strengthening Relationships: Practicing compassion fosters healthier and more genuine relationships, based on mutual understanding and respect.

Compassion for others helps rebuild the emotional bridges that The Hidden Wound of Rejection once broke. It is a path to forgiveness and the restoration of inner peace.

Both self-compassion and compassion for others have a direct impact on overcoming The Hidden Wound of Rejection:

- Reconfiguration of Emotional Patterns: Compassion dissolves cycles of pain and criticism, making way for new patterns based on love, understanding, and acceptance.

- Emotional Freedom: It allows you to leave behind hurt and feelings of inadequacy, creating space for a lighter and more meaningful life.
- Strengthening Identity: Compassion helps rebuild your emotional identity, enabling you to see yourself and others with greater clarity and less judgment.

Practicing Compassion in Daily Life

Developing and cultivating compassion requires intention and practice. Here are some ways to incorporate it into your journey:

Self-Compassion

- Practice Positive Self-Talk: When faced with self-critical thoughts, ask yourself: "*Would I say this to a dear friend?*"
- Create Moments of Self-Care: Dedicate time to caring for yourself, recognizing that you deserve kindness and attention.
- Self-Compassion Meditation: Visualize yourself sending thoughts of love and acceptance to your own wounds.

- Cultivate Active Listening: Be present when hearing others' stories or concerns, without judgment or interruption.
- Practice Small Acts of Kindness: A simple gesture, such as a word of support or a smile, can create deeper connections.
- Expand Your Perspective: Try to put yourself in someone else's shoes before reacting to a situation.

The Importance of Continuing to Cultivate Compassion

The continuous practice of compassion is essential to sustaining the transformation you have achieved so far. It helps prevent relapses into old emotional patterns, promotes resilience in the face of new challenges, and strengthens your ability to live in harmony with yourself and others.

Every act of compassion—whether toward yourself or others—is a step toward emotional freedom and the consolidation of your new self. By continuing to develop compassion, you not only free yourself from the weight of the past but also open yourself to a more connected, lighter, and meaningful life.

Compassion is the key to transforming pain into learning, self-criticism into acceptance, and disconnection into empathy. Cultivate it, practice it, and allow it to guide you at every step of this journey of healing and growth.

19

FORGIVENESS

Through the continuous practice of compassion, you begin to access an even deeper capacity for healing and transformation: forgiveness. Forgiveness is the ultimate release, an act that transcends pain and hurt, dissolving the chains that bind you to traumatic events and negative emotions. It is not a sign of weakness but an act of courage and strength, allowing you to leave behind the weight of the past and fully embrace the present.

Both self-forgiveness and forgiving others are fundamental in overcoming the hidden wound of rejection. When this feeling originates from intensely traumatic events, forgiveness becomes indispensable, as it is the only tool capable of breaking the chain that links you to such events and restoring the emotional freedom you seek.

The Eternity of a Moment

The phrase "*the eternity of a moment*" is often used in romantic contexts, where lovers wish to freeze in time moments of pure love. But have you ever stopped to think that, throughout life, we eternalize various moments? Curiously, most of these moments are not of joy but of trauma. And this is not our fault—it is part of our original programming.

The human brain, in its primary function, was designed to record painful events as a survival strategy. In the early days of our evolutionary history, when our interaction with the world was dictated by the dynamics of hunter and prey, this function was crucial. Our brain needed to quickly identify what posed a threat and how to avoid it in the future. Thus, experiences that threatened our physical integrity were recorded indelibly so they would never be forgotten. After all, remembering that certain plants were poisonous or that predators lurked in specific areas meant the difference between life and death.

This ability to record threatening events remains present in the modern human brain. The problem is that it does not distinguish between physical and emotional threats—it treats both as real dangers. For example, when you first touched fire and burned yourself, your brain permanently recorded that experience. You do not constantly relive that pain, but the memory serves as a defense mechanism: you simply will not put your hand in fire again.

Now, think about the impact of emotional pain. When something deeply hurt you—a word, a rejection, or abandonment—that experience was also recorded and may have been eternalized by your emotions. But unlike the burn, which creates a memory you effortlessly avoid, emotional pain from highly traumatic events enters an infinite loop. The brain, unable to fully process these experiences, can keep you trapped in suffering, reactivating that pain every time a similar situation arises.

In such cases, the most powerful tool is forgiveness. Forgiveness is not just an altruistic act; it is the key to breaking the cycle of suffering generated by eternalized moments of pain.

Forgiving does not mean forgetting or justifying what happened. It is a process of release. By forgiving, you acknowledge that the painful moment belongs to the past and that keeping it alive in the present only perpetuates suffering. You understand that, at the time of the trauma, you did not have the emotional tools and knowledge you possess now. But today, with greater clarity and maturity, you can use forgiveness as an antidote to untie the emotional knots that bind you to the past.

Think of forgiveness as a tool that allows you to reprogram your mind, transforming the pain of a traumatic moment into learning. When you practice forgiveness, you:

- Free yourself from the weight of the past: Forgiveness dissolves the emotional burden associated with the traumatic event.
- Regain control: Instead of allowing pain to dictate how you live, you take charge of your narrative.
- Create space for new experiences: By letting go of pain, you open space to fully live in the present and build a lighter future.

As challenging as forgiveness may be, it is an act of self-love. It is recognizing that you deserve to live without the burden of events that, although limited in time, have been eternalized in your mind.

Every moment you have eternalized has the power to shape your life, but it is up to you to choose how it will impact you. Using forgiveness to close cycles of pain is the necessary path to open yourself to new, lighter, and more meaningful experiences.

So, look within, recognize the moments your emotions have eternalized, and make the decision to release them. Forgiveness is the bridge that connects the past to the present, allowing you to move forward, stronger and freer than ever before.

Self-Forgiveness

Recognizing, Embracing and Releasing

For many, self-forgiveness may be the most challenging step, but it is also the most transformative. When the hidden wound of rejection is present, it is common to internalize guilt or believe that we are undeserving of love, acceptance, or happiness. Self-forgiveness redefines this concept:

- Recognizing personal limitations: Forgiving yourself is acknowledging that, like any human being, you are imperfect, prone to mistakes, and influenced by circumstances often beyond your control.
- Breaking the cycle of self-punishment: The practice of self-forgiveness dissolves harsh self-criticism and creates space for a healthier relationship with yourself, based on acceptance and self-compassion.

- Strengthening self-esteem: By forgiving yourself, you validate your humanity and reinforce your dignity, building a solid foundation for emotional reconstruction.

Self-forgiveness is an act of self-love, essential for freeing yourself from internal wounds that perpetuate the cycle of rejection.

Forgiving Others

Releasing the Burden of Resentment

When the hidden wound of rejection is linked to traumatic events, forgiving those who caused or contributed to these traumas may seem impossible. However, forgiving others is not about justifying or forgetting what happened; it is about freeing yourself from the influence these events have over your life:

- Breaking the chain of pain: Forgiveness severs the emotional connection to the traumatic event, allowing you to regain control over your life.
- Reducing resentment: Resentment is a burden that consumes your emotional energy. Forgiveness dissolves this weight, creating space for new emotions and experiences.
- Promoting reconnection: Though reestablishing relationships is not always necessary, forgiveness can help you see others with more compassion, humanizing those who caused you pain.

Forgiving others is an act of personal liberation—more for you than for those you forgive.

Forgiveness is a Journey, Not an Event

Forgiving—whether yourself or others—is not a linear or immediate process. It is a journey that requires patience, practice, and intention. Often, it happens in layers, as new insights and understandings emerge:

- Compassion as the foundation: Compassion is the basis of forgiveness. By understanding the circumstances and limitations that led you or others to certain behaviors, forgiveness becomes more accessible.
- Acknowledging the pain: Before forgiving, it is important to fully recognize the pain you felt, validating your emotions without judgment.
- Intentional choice: Forgiveness is a conscious choice, a deliberate act of letting go of pain and resentment to free yourself emotionally.

Practicing Forgiveness Daily

Like compassion, forgiveness requires continuous practice. Some ways to cultivate it include:

Self-Forgiveness

- Write to yourself: List your guilt and forgive yourself for each, recognizing your effort and courage in growing.
- Practice positive affirmations: Remind yourself daily that you are worthy of love, acceptance, and happiness, regardless of past mistakes.
- Meditate on self-acceptance: Visualize yourself surrounded by light, releasing the guilt that binds you.

Forgiving Others

- Practice emotional detachment: Separate the person from the act, focusing on forgiving the person's humanity, not necessarily their actions.
- Write letters of forgiveness: Even if you never send them, expressing your feelings and intentions in writing can be healing.
- Seek broader perspectives: Reflect on the factors that may have led the person to act the way they did—not to justify, but to understand.

Forgiveness as the Ultimate Liberation

Forgiving does not erase the past, but it dissolves the power it holds over you. It is an act of courage, love, and compassion that paves the way for a lighter and more meaningful life. In cases of hidden rejection, where deep traumas have left lasting scars, forgiveness is the bridge that transforms suffering into freedom, allowing you to fully embrace your new self.

Keep practicing forgiveness. It is not just the closing of a chapter but the key to a future free from the weight of the past and filled with emotional and relational possibilities. To forgive is to give yourself the opportunity to start anew.

20

NEW HORIZONS

On my personal journey of self-discovery, through countless repetitions of these exercises, I came to deeply understand how the hidden wound of rejection had shaped and influenced my life. I believe that the few personal accounts I've shared here are enough to give you a clear idea of this impact. Throughout this process, I revisited and relived moments and experiences that, on their own, could fill the pages of several other books.

The result of my honesty and courage in confronting my EGO has been, in many ways, profoundly rewarding. Seeing the happiness and inspiration on my wife's and my child's faces as they witness my mental reprogramming is something I never imagined achieving—even in my boldest dreams. Feeling the lightness in my thoughts and emotions, the peace of mind I have experienced since my first reframing exercises, is also something I never thought possible.

Today, I can look back at my past and, instead of feeling frustration, hurt, resentment, sadness, or even anger, I feel clarity, understanding, empathy, gratitude, and love. This unleashes a life force so powerful that, no matter how hard I try to put it into words, I can never fully express what I feel. It's like becoming a child again and rediscovering, deep in my heart, the endless possibilities for fulfillment that lie ahead.

You've made it this far, and that alone is a great victory. According to statistics, 90% of people who buy a book never read it. So, if you're here now, you are part of the select 10% who do. Congratulations! And thank you!

With the continued practice of the transformative techniques you've learned throughout this book, you may have already felt a profound shift: the hidden wound of rejection no longer controls your life. Those defense mechanisms that once drained your energy—leaving you with a constant sense of exhaustion, as if carrying the weight of the world on your shoulders—are no longer necessary. What once imprisoned you has now been undone, and you can finally breathe with lightness and freedom.

This liberation is not just emotional but also energetic. By breaking free from the chains of the past, you have discovered something powerful: your brain is programmable, and you have the power to reprogram it however you choose. This realization is the key to creating a new life—one free from the limitations imposed by fear, pain, and insecurity.

Now is the time to look ahead. Do you remember those dreams and projects that had been tucked away, gathering dust in the back of your mind? This is the moment to reclaim them. Take them out, revise them, and bring them to life with the renewed energy you now possess. But don't stop there! It's also time to reflect on everything life still has to offer and on the new paths that now unfold before you.

The walls that once limited your vision have been torn down. The landscape has changed, and with it, ***new horizons*** have emerged. These horizons represent infinite possibilities—a world full of experiences, achievements, and moments that you are now ready to embrace fully.

YOU ARE IN CONTROL OF YOUR LIFE

With courage, determination, and the tools you now possess, it's time to embrace your true potential. You are not defined by the pain of your past but by the strength and wisdom you have gained in overcoming it.

Life is ahead of you.
LIVE!

Fill yourself with enthusiasm, celebrate your victories, and take the next step with confidence. You are not just closing a book—you are beginning a new journey, where the only limits are those set by your imagination and your will to achieve.

New horizons await you.
Go beyond. Discover yourself.
And live intensely!

To learn more, visit:
www.gersondorneles.com

www.ingramcontent.com/pod-product-compliance
Ingram Content Group UK Ltd.
Pitfield, Milton Keynes, MK11 3LW, UK
UKHW041635190726
13854UKWH00006B/2509

9 786501 386362